Love
HAS NO
BORDERS

TRUE STORIES OF DESPERATION
AS SEEN BY A SOCIAL WORKER

*Lisa + Dave
Thank you for all you
do for others! God
Bless! Phyllis D*

PHYLLIS YVONNE DODD, LCSW

ISBN 978-1-64468-139-8 (Paperback)
ISBN 978-1-64468-140-4 (Digital)

Covenant Books, Inc.
11661 Hwy 707
Murrells Inlet, SC 29576
www.covenantbooks.com

"This is my story—or should I say, the story of people of different lands, who I see as all children of God and our 'neighbors'." Phyllis' words here sum up this very engaging piece of writing from a person whose life has embodied an expansive view of who is included under the term "neighbor"—a perspective needed as much today as it ever has been.

David Radcliff
Director, New Community Project

This is a marvelous account of how a professional social worker combines the ethics of a professional with the spiritual underpinnings of love, respect, and compassion for everyone.

The book provides critical lessons for understanding the human needs that are the same for everyone within the contexts of cultural and social justice.

Every social work program should designate **Love Has No Borders** *as required reading for every social work student.*

Marlene A. Saunders, DSW, LMSW

Dedicated to Paul who shared his love
for peace and justice
in the world

*We have gained a hundredfold from the refugees;
we have been thinking that we have given so
much to the refugees who have come in, but
they have given us hundredfold instead.*
—Eleanor Roosevelt

CONTENTS

PREFACE

I wondered why I was so interested in working with people from other countries and discovering other lands. Was it because our family traveled each summer on family vacations and to conferences, allowing me to visit almost every state in the United States as a child? My mother said that I probably inherited it from my great-grandparents who would load up their six children in a Model T and travel to nearby states in the early '30s. I have always had such a great curiosity of other people and customs in other lands, so perhaps that is why it was only natural that I would want to travel and meet people from other countries.

I remember as a little girl in elementary school, our Brownie troop went to a May Day celebration and saw children from all over the world dance their native dances around the maypole. I was fascinated! I remember asking my mother, who was the Girl Scout leader at the time, if I would be able to travel all over the world someday, and she said that, sometimes, Girl Scouts travel to other countries. So I decided then that I would set that as a goal and stayed in Girl Scouts so that I could one day visit other lands.

I remember going to Youth Life Lab and Camp Woodland Alters and meeting African students. We tried to learn some of their language. I also dreamed of visiting Africa and loved to hear the spoken language.

We studied the pyramids of Egypt in sixth grade and then I decided I wanted to go to Egypt. We studied astronomy in sixth grade, and I decided I wanted to be an astronaut and travel to the moon. Well, that did not happen.

I decided I wanted to learn German, so I got a record and a book and tried to teach myself German, but that ended when we were caring for our neighbor's German poodle, and the beloved dog accidently got run over in front of our house. That haunted me for a long time.

Then my parents started receiving foster children into the home. We hosted several children for relatively short periods of time. Having foster children living with us soon turned into sponsoring exchange students, and we soon became a part of a student exchange program, with my brother going to Guatemala and a Guatemalan student coming to live with us. My brother spent several weeks in Guatemala and then a Guatemalan student came to stay with us for a while.

I have always told people later that this was the real reason that I wanted to learn Spanish! Even though he called me *gordita*, I decided I would learn the Spanish language. I would take him with me to high school, and he would sit in with me in my Spanish class. That soon ended when he continuously corrected my Spanish teacher, which made her very upset. This was the beginning of my goal of learning Spanish! *Hola, ¿Que tal? ¿Como Estás? ¿Bien, y tú?* I still remember the first page of that book.

I studied Spanish for several years and chose to go to Juniata College which was the perfect school for me because it required very little math, which was not one of my strong points, and we were able to write our own program of studies. I decided, without a doubt, that I wanted to attempt a double major of Social Work and Spanish.

In my junior year of college, I joined Brethren Colleges Abroad and spent one school year in Barcelona, Spain. This was 1979, the year that Franco had died, and the country was in turmoil, hoping to restore the *Catalán* culture and a language which had been forbidden for so many years. I loved the experience of spending the summer as a tour guide on the island of Ibiza (Balearic Islands) and brought back many stories of adventures of that summer. I dreamed of becoming a hippie, and so I dressed up as a hippie on Paradise Island and gave tours to the European tourists visiting the island. I also did this *without a work permit*, getting paid cash! So I also had that experience preparing me for my future work with undocumented immigrants in the United States. At least, I can say I've been an undocumented immigrant in another country, working illegally and trying hard to learn a second language. Learning a second language is not that easy! But what a wonderful time that was, and I did eventually return to the United States.

After college, I joined the Peace Corps as a community promoter and was placed in Ecuador, South America. I was going to go to Honduras, but the war in Central America had just started, so the area was too dangerous. I had a wonderful experience for the year that I lived in Ecuador and felt that I was finally able to master the Spanish language.

I came back to the United States, and after working several short-term temporary jobs, I worked with Church World Service, processing Cuban "entrants" from Mariel, who had found themselves to our country by way of boat. Our country considered them mentally ill and criminals who were let out of the prisons there. I found myself defending them constantly, stating that they were just lost souls trying to find their way into a new culture. They were just regular people who had just been placed in jail for stealing an orange or some other product on the black market.

It was extremely difficult for them to become acculturated into the society of the United States, and I soon learned that it was a fact that many were mentally ill, men and women who were released from the prisons and mental health institutions of Cuba. I still treated them with respect and care because *who else was going to help them through resettlement, relocation, and job placement?* The experience for me was invaluable as I was learning the Spanish language well and was even told that I had a Cuban accent. That was a huge compliment for me, being *gringa* and all.

I also became very involved with the church and the peace stance of the Church of the Brethren. I would attend conferences and retreats with my family and then my husband. I became active with Brethren Peace Fellowship and came to know Dale and Ruth Aukerman, who were instrumental in validating and developing my faith walk. I soon learned the discrepancies of other Christians, who did not necessarily hold the same beliefs that I did, about peace and justice in the world. That confused me to no end. How could that be? Aren't we, as Christians, called to love and care for our brothers and sisters all over the world? Does it not say,

> Then they also will answer, "Lord, when was it that we saw you hungry or thirsty or a stranger or naked or sick or in prison, and did not take care of you?" Then he will answer them, "Truly I tell you, just as you did not do it to one of the least of these, you did not do it to me." (Matthew 25:44–45, NRSV)

So this is my story—or should I say, the story of people of different countries, who I see as all children of God and our "neighbors." We are living with them in this universe, we are all *one*, we are on this earth together, and we need to help others as we would want to be helped. We would want to "do unto others as we would have them do unto us." We want to welcome others as we would want to be welcomed. We would want to help the newcomer integrate into society and find a job so that that they may feed their children and families just as we would want to feed our own children and families. If we treat someone poorly or reject another person in need, we are only hurting ourselves because we are they, and they are we. We need to refuse to "harm" ourselves and our planet. We are called to love our neighbor as ourselves, and that means even our enemies. Some so-called Christians believe that they are only called to help those in their hometown or those who "look like them." They believe in the death penalty, punishment, vengeance, war, and judgment. Is that really what the Bible teaches?

Yes, it is challenging to be a Christian in our times. And this is why I wanted to write this book. I wanted to tell the stories of real people from different lands and their reasons for coming to our country—our communities—and our towns. They are people with a real heart and soul like us. They have become our next-door neighbors in many cases. What are you called to do about this? We can welcome them or reject them, but I choose to welcome them because if I was in their situation, I would bless those who would welcome me as I believe Jesus calls us to do.

I want to tell the stories from different cultures that I have worked with in my life as a social worker. I have had the privilege of meeting so many beautiful individuals. I have met with refugees, entrants, immigrants, families, and children of several countries. I have also worked with the victims of crime as well as perpetrators of domestic violence and criminals. I consider them our "neighbors" and our "brothers and sisters." More than often, those who are angry and violent and hurting the worst are the very ones who are the neediest, the ones who have suffered in their own lives—we do not know. We are not to judge. We do not know the path they have followed unless we get to know them. So how do we treat the stranger?

Another important aspect of this book is to understand that no matter how cruel the world is, there are good people in the world, and there is help there for those who suffer. We may have government leaders in our country who govern by use of power and control, but I always have believed that love is more powerful than hate and greed, and that love *will* prevail. Maybe this is a test for us, to see if we are strong enough to welcome a person who suffers. These are real stories of people seeking refuge in the United States. They are not all good stories, but they are real stories of people who have suffered and fled for their lives. I hope that others can experience a message of hope and encouragement from these stories.

I pray that the general public can finally understand that everyone has a history. Each person has a story to tell, and as we look at others, we will not know the history until we ask them to tell their story. They are fellow human beings seeking refuge and protection from tragedy, trauma, starvation, war, natural disasters, and the list could go on and on.

I have heard the stories of hundreds of individuals seeking asylum in the United States. I have provided therapy to hundreds of families and children who have been traumatized, and I have interviewed hundreds of individuals who have applied for visas and asylum, hoping to remain in the United States. These evaluations are submitted to immigration and then to judges who are making important decisions about the future lives of many men, women, and children. These judges have such an important job to do and must be commended.

I want to thank all of those who allowed me to use their story. Names and even some locations have been changed as to protect the identity of each person; however, these are true stories and true experiences.

INTRODUCTION

Curing Desperation

This is an article that came out of the *Washington Post* on October 18, 1981, Outlook Section, by Marlene Sokol, copied with permission.

A black heavyset Cuban man of 50 sat in front of my desk and frowned thoughtfully. "*Como voy hacer esto* (How do I do this)?" he asked.

"Do what?" I looked down at the bill of $323.00 from the local C&P telephone company. "You send them a check."

"A what?"

"A check or money order. To this amount."

The man laughed faintly and shuffled the computer card around in his large, clumsy hands. "What is that? Can you do it for me?"

I held my breath and tapped my fingers on the desk. "How did you pay your bill last month?"

"That woman did it for me."

"What woman?"

"My neighbor, the one who was in with me last week."

"Does she pay your phone bill for you every month?"

"She has to…you have to…What do I know about all this? I'm going to lose my phone…"

"Look, all you have to do is to go to a post office…" The man was on his feet, shaking his head as he stuffed the enveloped into his pocket and glanced around the office for another social worker.

In one more week, my housing counseling days will be over. Once more, I will be unemployed, another BA in liberal arts trying to break down doors and get by secretaries in the who-do-you-know city of Washington, DC. But after ten months and a lot of close calls with my clients, the authorities, and even my coworkers, I have realized that I am just not social-worker material.

Yes, there really is a prototype "social worker." Take Yvonne, for example. Yvonne is a Christian, and perhaps that is why she never gets frustrated or gives up. Yvonne has been robbed and taken advantage of more times that I can count. Yet she looks forward to coming to work in the morning, to chauffeuring able-bodied men to the welfare office, and to finding jobs for people who have already lost six or seven jobs gotten for them by Yvonne. She is the only one in the office who has patience for Laura, the hysterical football player of a woman who haunts our office day and night. For some reason, Laura never receives her welfare checks or her food stamps and is always starving to death. But her landlord claims she receives at least three male visitors per night.

Or look at Alba. Alba has never uttered a negative word about anyone in the nine months I have known her, even though she is grossly underpaid and constantly chewed out by the director. I remember one rainy day in March, when one of her clients, a youth of 21, stood trembling over her desk.

"My landlord's trying to evict me," he shouted.

"Please try to lower your voice," Alba warned quietly.

"Look, if I have to go back to sleeping in the car, I'll shoot myself." The young man drew a .38 caliber out of his pocket and held it to his head. "I mean it. I'll shoot myself right here in this office."

"Now, just calm down," said Alba. "There's no need of that. Just let me have a talk with your landlord." As it turned out, the tenant only owed one month's rent and late fees. (Marlene Sokol, Outlook section, *Washington Post*, Oct. 18, 1981)

The above was a true-life article written in the *Washington Post* about the office where I worked in Silver Spring, Maryland. I had landed a job, first working with Church World Service through the resettlement of Cuban refugees at Fort Indiantown Gap and then I was hired by the local agency (Spanish Speaking Community of Maryland) that was helping the refugees with resettlement. There was an earlier influx of Cubans who had entered the country between 1959 and 1970 who became very successful in the United States, but this was a totally different group of people who were needy and visited our office frequently. I loved the job, but obviously, it was not for everyone. These were the Cubans that had come into Mariel, Key West, Florida, in 1980.

I also decided to use my middle name, Yvonne, as my first name because the clients could not say Phyllis. I was being called many other names, including Philips or Felix, so I began my new career with this alias and have been using it ever since.

I'm not sure why I added this article as an introduction, except to remember what it was like for me almost forty years ago. I was a young social worker, some would say naive, who truly cared about everyone that came across my desk. It has been like that for me for years and still is. As the Cubans entered the country, the press talked bad about the newcomers and accused them of being criminals and mentally ill. I worked with approximately 700 Cubans that year, assisting in the resettlement process for each of them. I saw each person as an individual with a problem—that of escaping their country—who needed assistance in a new country. I was not going to judge their reasons for coming here, but that deep down, they wanted a chance. They were here to stay and needed to learn the ins and outs of this country that was totally different from where they had come from.

I consider myself to be lucky to have been born into the United States, not rich but having everything I need to get by—a job, an education, and food on the table. I have family and friends and a church family. I live in a society where our police, first responders, firemen, and yes, even politicians, are doing their best to take care of this country (except for those who we know are only interested in their egos). I always try to put myself in their shoes.

Refugees and immigrants, entrants and refugees are coming from other countries. Many are not as fortunate as we are. I have heard people from Central America say that just by the fact that we are American, we are all powerful. It is called *privilege*. We have money at our fingertips, and the streets are lined with gold. They believe we can do anything, and we can accomplish anything if we want to, and often, that is the case. Some of you may not believe that, but perhaps, we have been born into this country so that we can make a difference in the world, either one person at a time or to a total country. It all depends on how you look at things. So many feel that they are powerless, but if you want to accomplish something, and you put your mind to it, you can. God has put us on this earth for a purpose. What is your purpose? What do you want to be remembered for?

Yes, I have been robbed, taken advantage of, and lied to. But I am okay, and I can survive. So what can I do to be an example for those who are less fortunate? This book will tell you about my experiences as a social worker, working with people from several different countries, including Americans. Each person comes from a different walk of life. I hope that it may inspire you, in some way, or at least help you understand why we are called to "do unto others as we would have them do unto us." Remember, what would *you* do if you were in their shoes?

You are a tool in the hands of God. He
demands your service, not your rest, yet,
how fortunate you are that He lets you
take part in His work! (Ulrich Zwingli,
father of the Swiss Reformation)

CHAPTER 1

Los Marielitos, 1980–1983

At that time, I was working with the Cuban entrants (or *Marielitos* as they were commonly called). In 1980, roughly 124,779 Cubans migrated to the United States from Mariel.[1] Thus by 1982, the United States population of Cuban origin was approaching the one-million mark. At that time, Dade County, Florida, was the undisputed center of the Cuban community in this country, with more than 50 percent of United States Cubans residing there. Sizable Cuban colonies also existed in New Jersey, New York, California, Illinois, Texas, and Puerto Rico. Now the Cubans were being relocated into the Pennsylvania and Maryland area as well as other states.

According to Magaly Queralt, the Cubans made up the third largest Hispanic subgroup, after Mexicans and Puerto Ricans (Understanding Cuban Immigrants—A Cultural Perceive. NASW, Inc.).[2] The Cuban population who came in 1980 was an overrepresentation of criminals and other institutionalized persons forced or persuaded to leave.

I had heard that this group was much different than the Cubans who had immigrated in 1959, shortly after Fidel Castro's assumption

[1] Batalove, J. and Zong, Jie, "Migration Information Source, Cuban Entrants in the United States," November 9, 2017, source@migrationpolicy.org

[2] Queralt, Magaly, National Association of Social Workers, Inc., "Understanding Cuban Immigrants—A Cultural Perspective," pg. 115, 1984.

of power. Cubans arriving during the earlier wave of immigrants were coming from Cuba for reasons other than economic reasons such as those from Mexico or Puerto Rico. Most of the earlier Cubans were political refugees motivated by a lack of adaptation to the culture. They were lawyers, doctors, teachers, carpenters, masons, and bricklayers, all willing to work at minimum wage or below. These people were assisted in every way to become adjusted in the United States. Small business loans, special education programs and grants for American universities and other special services helped make the adjustment of these Cubans more successful than the members of any other of the waves of immigrants. These people knew deprivation, repression, and submission in Cuba because of the change of policies and, for this reason, reacted differently than the wave of 1980.

But this wave of Cuban refugees (later to be named "entrants") was supposedly being freed from the jails and the mental institutions.

I began to work in resettlement efforts with these *Marielitos* (Cubans from 1980) at Ft. Indiantown Gap as an interviewer and link for each individual and family to reconnect with family or relatives in the United States. I did this for two months and, for the following three years, worked as a social worker in a small organization working with the Latino community in the heart of Takoma Park Maryland. It was hard for me to land that job in an agency that had never hired an American before. The organization was run by an older Cuban gentleman who was very much anti-Castro, and his mission was to use his politics to fight back from what he had grown up with in Cuba.

In 1980, I had just returned from South America, where I was trying so hard to learn the Spanish language. Someone had told me that when I could "dream" in Spanish, this meant that I had finally integrated the language. It took a long time, but I had finally dreamt in Spanish while in Ecuador! I wanted to get into my field of social work, working with Latino folks, which is why I wanted to learn Spanish.

I was working in Washington, DC, doing a "filing" job when I had just earned my college degree. I felt out of place and was unhappy that I was not doing the social work that I dreamed of doing. I was working with high-class, well-dressed entrepreneurs and felt out of place among the "fashion show" that was walking down the street day after day. I had to ride on the metro, which was not all that bad because as I went in, I had the ability to fall asleep by the second metro stop and then wake up at my destination stop. I would walk among the hundreds of preppy adults who were trying to make an impression in the DC scene, and I loathed it. Did they not understand that so many people in the world were suffering?

I went to work at the Helicopter Association of America and, later, the Travel Association of America where I was placed through a temp organization. Why was I placed in those agencies? Because I had told the temp agency that I wanted a "travel" job. Oh well, I never did get to travel, only imagined that I was going somewhere.

One day, I walked in the boss's office and confessed that I was so unhappy there. I told him that I would like to either get paid more to do the same boring work I was doing, change my job to something more interesting or to a helping profession where I could use my education in Social Work, or quit.

The employer asked me, "If you could do anything, what would you do?"

I said, "I want to use my Spanish and social work education and work at the community center in Takoma Park, Maryland, where I can use these skills."

He told me to go. "You need to do what you really want to do." He said he would give me two weeks of severance pay, and I should go to that agency to volunteer for two weeks, in which time, they should be giving me a permanent job, and then I would be on my way. I did just that and never felt freer in my whole life!

I went to volunteer at the agency for two weeks, but they did not have a contract yet for work with the Cubans, so they told me I would have to wait. Then God answered my prayers, and I was called by Church World Service.

"We heard that you speak Spanish and would like to know if you could work at the processing center at Ft. Indiantown Gap, Pennsylvania, for the summer?"

"Of course, I will!"

25

In my diary, I wrote,

I packed my bag and hurried up to the army barracks where I was given a room. The rooms were small and hot as there was no air conditioning. Where I lived overlooked the single male barracks which was guarded by guards twenty-four hours a day. Still, the women workers get whistled at as we drove up the hill—just like any Spanish country. It was also a reminder of my old room in Alluriquin (Ecuador) because it's small and wooded, and outside, Spanish salsa music was blasting on a record player. Movies were going on every night—*Kung Fu,* etc. You can hear people singing, clapping, etc. I love it here. I had my tape player and guitar with me but spent every day processing families and individuals.

I loved my job, and I wrote,

They looked so desolate, and they all have soft eyes and scared eyes. I feel like it's up to me to release them out from this jailhouse. Just the look they give me seemed to say, *Please help!*

One experience that happened today, Raul, who was a clean-cut man, came in. He looked so sad when he told me his wife and two children were still in Cuba. He came in and begged me, "*Por favor*! Please help me and my family! I can't remember my brother's telephone number, and I don't know who else to call. Please help me find a sponsor!"

He was so happy when I told him he had a sponsor and could leave soon! If he didn't already have a sponsor, I would have had the church sponsor him. Well, he left, came back later, and asked me if I had change for a dollar. I didn't quite but borrowed a dime from a friend. Well, ten minutes later, he comes back to my desk, set a Coke on it, and walked out. I had a client there and did not know what to say, and he never turned around. I could have cried because I thought that was a special act of kindness.

At the same time, there was an old man there—black, with white hair, no English, no sponsor. I don't know what we will be able to do with him here in the United States. He does look like someone out of the prison—but also had sad eyes like, *What will happen to me now?*

Up on the wall, there was a sign that said "Human Resources." We jokingly said, "Inhuman Resources."

It was so hot and sticky, and I drank cold Mellow Yellow soda all day long! The refugees were begging me to interview them first, and they were desperate to leave the barracks.

I did just that, working at Ft. Indiantown Gap, interviewing the Cubans and matching them with sponsors all over the United States. It was exciting to listen to so many stories of men and women and watching families come through, desperately seeking distant relatives in the United States, and trying to link them with sponsors all over the United States. This was where my Spanish began to flourish.

One day, a man came in, ragged and very thin. His name was Ramón, and he seemed tired, but he wanted to tell me about his country, so I asked him what it was like in Cuba. He told me that he used to be a cook, and he would earn 163 pesos a month for a family of four.

"My brother was a painter, and he only earned 127 pesos a month. It costs 30 pesos for a bad pair of jeans and 100 pesos for a good pair of jeans that you can buy on the black market. A T-shirt costs 125 pesos, and a pair of shoes costs 100 pesos. There is not enough for my family, and I actually only receive 72 pesos for every 100 pesos earned. There are four people in my family, and we all lived in one room. If you want to build a house and start to build, they will make you tear it down."

Ramón added, "The food rations for a family of four include four pounds of rice a month, two pounds of beans a month, four pounds of sugar a person per month, one and a half pounds of lard per person per month, two cans of puree per family per month, one blanket per month, one razor blade every two months, one pair of shoes per person per year, and one pair of boots for work per person per year. Each person has a ticket book with rations. Each time they go to the store, they hand over a ticket with the money.

"I knew a person who was thrown in jail for having a Bible. I had to leave my children and everything behind. I am tired and discouraged."

If that does not remind you of a Bible verse, I don't know what does.

At home, I could just imagine my family and friends thinking, *That crazy girl, doesn't know what she is doing and does not know when to stop.* They are right. And I'm not going to stop dreaming either, and this is exactly where I belong. I feel good about it. I would like to continue the dream.

Another day, I went out to the barracks to visit a family with another worker. There was a most beautiful family there. They even had blond hair and hazel eyes. The fifteen-year-old girl was beautiful. Well, come to find out this family already has a house waiting for them in Chicago and a church for the father to preach at. I was sitting there conversing with them, and I had to ask them if they knew any other family without a sponsor. They pointed out a short dark-skinned woman who was sitting in the same room, who did not say anything but was trying to hide her eyes which had tears streaming out of them. She cried, and no one said anything.

"Do you know anyone in the United States?"

"No," she said.

"No one?"

"No. I do not have anyone."

I took her name and number, and my mission was to find a sponsor for her. I felt so sorry for her that I could have cried myself. She needed somewhere to go.

The refugee camp where I was looked all right, considering. The rooms were neat, and you could tell the ones who had relatives that had visited because there were pillows, shampoo, extra baby food, etc. One family was moving out and had all kinds of items. The people were just dying to leave. The minister said it was terrible because some of the single men and women were being moved in closer to the families with children. He said the women practically wore nothing, and he knew there were convicts and homosexuals mixed into the crowd. He said he hated to take his children to the mess hall to eat because of all the bad language that went on there. I wanted to cry.

And I wrote,

> I interviewed a homosexual yesterday—a man who had long painted fingernails and jewelry. Interviewing him made me examine my own beliefs, and I felt a little uncomfortable. But this experience is making me a stronger, and I know that my fate is in God's hands and that with His blessing, I will learn to be a better caregiver and counselor. I pray that I become a better Christian. I pray also that Paul (my future husband) and I can come to talk about these kinds of issues with each other.
>
> The next day, I went back to the interviewing room and, in the background, could hear the Spanish/Cuban music blaring, and on top of that, a man was playing the trumpet. Outside, there was lightning and thunder, but there was no rain. It was almost like daytime because you could see the mountain in the back. The trumpet player was excellent. He must have been a professional in Cuba; no bad notes or anything. Then

it just started raining and pouring. I had bought a little fan to help keep me cool and sat there listening to the rain and thinking about *living the simple life,* which is another goal I have set for myself. I love the sound of the rain on the roof; there is something very calming about it.

I decided at this time, that I was going to type up all my diaries that I had written in now for about eight years and write a book someday!

I saw a family leaving today and realized that I had just interviewed them about two days ago. That made me so happy to see them on their way. I interviewed about eight to ten more people today, and two of the men were highly educated, and so I sent them to the University of Pennsylvania, who were looking for Cuban refugees for their ESOL program and were willing to sponsor them. I also interviewed a family who had lost their son and another relative who were in another camp.

One day, there was a riot at the barracks, and we all had to be evacuated. The Cubans had begun to revolt as they thought that they were being held there against their will. I could tell that the people were getting more anxious. In the barracks, everyone was walking up and down the hallway, and the phones were ringing. The Cubans were having another "parade" and banging on tin cans and marching, singing and yelling. I was thinking, *I don't know what their intentions are. I just hope they don't come up here.*

Every time I went to the office, the refugees were asking me when they could leave. They kept asking the same questions over and over as if I could do anything for them in the middle of a riot, and it was starting to make me feel anxious. Everyone was tense. I could feel it in the air.

Then on August 5, 1980, we were working, but I was informed that we should *move out fast* if any of the Cubans break through. We were told that they had gotten into the mess halls and had taken all the knives. Later, we had to out-process a man that the other Cubans were threatening. He was the one that warned everybody to get out of the mess halls that morning. Well, at 5:00 p.m., we got word to evacuate the building because they were starting more riots. We did, and as I was leaving, I saw the army jeeps going by with soldiers lying down—hit. Everybody was yelling to get out, and it was scary.

I stayed away for a while, but had nowhere to go, so I tried to get a room at the women's barracks (they wouldn't let me because I was *just a civilian*!). We were told to stay away for a couple of days, and during that time, parts of the buildings were raided, including my room, destroying some of the property. I went to stay with some friends at a nearby town and waited until everything was clear to return. When I returned, I saw that my room had been broken into and was a wreck. I was so worried about my radio and guitar and *charango*, but someone had hidden all three things under the bed, and I guess they were overlooked. Thank goodness.

The refugees were so frustrated. They were desperate to be interviewed, and it was going so slow. They told me stories of the risky boat ride to Key West, and how some had even lost their lives. They told of the terrible life that they had lived, and the efforts to survive in their country. They would cry and yell and mostly plead for help to find a place to live.

But then there were the good stories of sponsorships. I interviewed a family with a mother, grandmother, little girl and boy, and the mother was crying. The children had been put into a holding area because of the riot. I did all I could to get them out and, finally, found out that we had found them a sponsor in Virginia through USCC. She left so happy. I took two pictures, which, I guess, I was not supposed to do because the military police took my film away! I was so upset.

I received a certificate from the Cuban-Haitian Task Force head, Ambassador Victor Palmieri, for "Meritorious Service in the Cuban Resettlement Program at Fort Indiantown Gap, Pennsylvania."

I returned to the Washington, DC, area and began working with the Cubans who were resettling through the same agency that I had hoped to work for. I was the first *gringa* who ever worked there! From October 1980 to September 1983, I worked with over 700 Cuban entrants who had settled in Montgomery County, Maryland. I spent days on end going back and forth to the hospitals as a translator, working with employers, working with landlords, translating for psychiatrists, accompanying police officers, translating in the court, and trying to help the Cubans become resettled in this country.

For the next three years, I continued work with the Cuban/Haitian Program right in the community, street level, with large glass windows. Through these windows, we not only could see into the heart of the community, but we also could see into the hearts of the people seeking refuge. These are some of the stories that I recorded during that time.

"Which of these three do you think was a
neighbor to the man who fell into the hands
of the robbers?" He said, "the one who
showed him mercy". Jesus said to him, "Go
and do likewise" (Luke 10:36-37). NRSV

CHAPTER 2

Stories of the Cuban Entrants

These are true accounts of my work with the Cubans of 1980–
1983. These excerpts come from a diary I kept for a few months
of working in this agency.

Carmen and Freddy had just found an
apartment and were going to live together "in
different rooms of course," they explained to me
as I started my day in a street-level office behind
all-glass windows. Pedro, a transvestite, had just
come into the office to drop off a picture of
himself (herself) in a flowing long pink gown.
About two hours later, he came into the office
to show the receptionist his pink toenails. Other
than that, the day was quiet. I was waiting for an
inspection for the Cuban Resettlement Program
at 9:00 a.m. and received word at 9:05 a.m.
that they could not make it. I had been doing
paperwork.

A word about Carmen and Freddy, since living in the United
States, Carmen had been in one crisis after another. Freddy claimed
she was mentally ill, and that in Cuba, she was in a mental hospital

where they had put electrodes in her head. Carmen told me that she had gotten married, had children, and so now her main goal in the United States was to earn money to send to her children and, eventually, bring them here to the States. However, after each crisis (or during), Carmen did not cooperate with anything or anyone. She was unemployed and, usually, would lose her apartment because of her inability to find a job, pay rent, and get along with others due to mental health problems. She often lived on the street and had been interviewed and been in the newspaper with a picture of her sleeping on a park bench. She moved from emergency shelter to emergency shelter. She usually could not resolve her problems and was arrested twice for yelling in various offices. The county police knew her well.

Often, the Cuban entrants I worked with would find themselves in this situation. Many of the entrants had come from mental facilities or jails and did not know how to find a job, keep a job, or to make a living. For the general population, it was explained to me that in Cuba, the housing was provided, and food staples were rationed. It was not surprising that they did not have the knowledge or know how to be self-sufficient.

Carmen would not look for a job even when desperately in need of an income. She would beg from door to door and was also arrested for this reason.

In some ways, Carmen did well. She was able to learn some English and worked well caring for an elderly woman. She had a nice personality when she was not upset. However, if she did not feel like working, she would just stop, lie down, and go to sleep. She demonstrated serious mental health problems and had been taken to the hospital several times for treatment but would not follow any of the treatment plans.

Freddy, on the other hand, seemed to move ten times a year. He was considered mentally disabled and was receiving SSI benefits as an eligible entrant. Because of the changes of address, he usually could not collect his benefits or housing and then he would come to the agency I worked at in these times of crisis. He would usually put on a scene and be thrown out of the Social Security office by police, therefore, agencies knew him well.

The Cuban *Marielitos* were in a class of their own. They were Cuban entrants, with a legal classification, and were able to receive these benefits that would help them get on their feet. This is not the case for those who are illegally entering the country; these immigrants never had access to benefits, contrary to many people's beliefs. After eighteen months, Cuban entrants could apply for residency, and in five years, they could apply for citizenship.

Even though Freddy seemed harmless to us at the agency, after getting to know him well, we found that he carried a knife around with him and had been thrown in jail for threatening someone on the bus in Washington, DC. He told me he only did this because someone kept telling him to turn down his radio, and he did not want to. Freddy was able to pay rent, but he was very hard to reason with.

I was told that part of Freddy's mental illness was his claim that when he walked down the street, he imagined all women that he looked at as completely nude. At the time, someone mentioned to me jokingly, "Well, that would include most men," which is not a good thought!

But this month, both Carmen and Freddy were on the street, and both claimed they could not live with any other person, so both decided to share an apartment. Rumors were they were in love, but I hardly doubt it. On February 4, 1983, Freddy and Carmen asked us to help them both move. I don't consider our agency a moving company, but the "boss" said to go ahead. Besides, I suppose we are a *support services agency*. Carmen was also in the process of applying for SSI.

February 7, 1983. Today was a very busy day. Juan L. had just left the office. He was the man who had bought a Volkswagen bug. He said three months ago, a taxi ran into the back of his car and still had not paid for the damages. He wanted a lawyer, and so I referred him to the community center next door that provided one free legal session with a lawyer per client.

I felt, since the very beginning, Juan L. could not be trusted, and by his looks alone, he still seemed to be a leery person. He claimed he was "a true Christian" and that this conversion had happened since coming to the United States. He told me that a nun had sponsored him out of the camp, and once he left, he went to Miami, came back to Maryland and then got a job right away at an apartment complex. From then on, after lectures about being a responsible person, Juan had come a long way. He landed a good job and improved his appearance. He always advised us of church meetings and how he was slowly learning the Bible.

Two other people who were improving every time I saw them had come into the office and were witnessing. They said they had been asked by their minister (Baptist) to go on a mission to Puerto Rico. I don't know why I was unsure of these stories, but who am I to decide what is true or not? I hoped it was true.

Later that day, Freddy called me to say that Carmen is a violent woman and started to complain about an argument over the heat. I told him that he and she were going to have to work these things out themselves and learn to resolve their problems between themselves. He was a little upset and said he was not going to come to me about that issue anymore.

On Tuesday, February 8, 1983, the inspection of this program was cancelled, so I called Keith Richburg who was a writer for the *Washington Post* to see if he wanted to do a story about the lives of these Cubans. He said maybe if I wrote a story about the lives of these Cubans, I could get some magazine to publish it, or even the *Washington Post*, and that has given me some incentive to write on.

And then there was Felipe, Angel, and Rogelio. These three men had come into the country together. Upon arrival, Felipe had started to live with a girl from the Philippines who did not know any Spanish, and of course, he knew no English. He explained to me a year later that she was abusing him and would not allow him to leave the house, would not allow him to work, and was very controlling. He said later that she would go to work every day, leaving him locked in the house. Later, he told me that she had a lot of money and was going to leave him a good fortune and go back to the Philippines. He was happy because then he would have the freedom to work.

His friend, Angel, lived with two different girls. One had left him when he was put in jail for the first time and then he got married to the other one. Felipe and Angel were taken in for questioning on the murder of their friend Rogelio, who had been stabbed seventeen times. They told me the story and how his eye had been poked out. I realize people lie every day, but I was completely perplexed about this one. This was extremely hard for me to believe, yet almost anything is possible coming from them.

Then Rogelio's girlfriend told me the whole story of the murder as she was making funeral arrangements for Rogelio. She said Felipe and Angel were the last ones seen with him and ended up with his car when it was all over. "Jefe" (my boss) advised me to stay out of it because he thought it was a drug deal, where some man from Miami had come to kill him. Felipe and Angel were eventually let free, and both said they had begun attending the Baptist church and claim they are turning to religion. I prayed that they would turn their lives around.

I really enjoy working with these people no matter how horrible it may seem. It is necessary to be cautious, yet I see the struggle that each one has and the time that each one needs. I could see working with each individual, taking into consideration their situations, and helping them integrate into the society, however, even *adult foster care* would have taken a long time with that process.

I believe that God has the power to make a difference in everyone's life, and that miracles happen. So many people that I meet seem so miserable and lost, but there is an answer. I pray that for so many people that I meet, that they might find peace in their lives.

Many Cubans entrants who I worked with were having a difficult time in adjusting to this culture. Some, like Carmen, Carlos, Freddy, and many others, are always changing addresses, always in a crisis situation, constantly losing their housing or their job, and ended up with no money. Then they throw their demands on people to help, and it becomes harder and harder to want to continue to help them, especially when you see the help you have given them did not work the first time.

Some of the Cubans that I had met, between the ages of thirty-five and fifty-five years old, had questionable educational levels, and you knew that they were not capable of making sound decisions. Their ignorance led them to ask me many questions, and they even wondered why they were in the situation they were in *again*. The culture that they came from also, whether it is the communist country that took care of all of their basic needs, OR the fact that they may have come from prison or a mental institution as the media proclaimed, made it very difficult to adjust to a new life. Everything was so foreign to them. I continued to try to explain new traditions, to teach them new ways of doing things, to counsel them, and sometimes, there was just not enough time.

Then there were the times when you have absolutely no pity on them and tell them to go to the TESS Community Center down the street. That left me feeling guilty, so I tried not to do it. On the other hand, the day you find that your client has finally begun to work, support themselves and pay rent, you feel like jumping for joy!

One day, as I reflected on all that had happened, Eduardo came in with a problem paying his rent. I asked where he was living.

He asked, "Can you please call my apartment manager, but don't tell her my name because I'm not supposed to be living there. Please ask her if I can pay (three months' rent) on the eighteenth."

"Who else is living there?" I asked.

He answered, "Jose (a fifty-five-year-old man), who pays me $100.00 a month so that he can use my address, but I do not know where he really is living."

Tell me if that isn't confusing!

Carmen was back over at Social Services demanding food stamps. I told her, "'Carmen, you have to be approved from your worker before you go to pick them up."

"It does not matter," she says. "The system isn't fair, and they should be there like others!"

There was no way to reason with Carmelina when she's hungry!

"Jefe" kept yelling about telephone lines, station wagon keys, gasoline, and the remodeling of the downstairs. Adela, another older Cuban woman with dark curly hair splattered with grey, called and said she went to my office again yesterday looking for me, and they told her I was not there. She was trying to find Social Services (different agency, different location). She was considered a "paranoid senile old woman who cries at everything." She kept asking me if it was okay what they had told her.

Reinaldo just called. Immigration had come here looking for him, but of course, we could not give them any information, and they would not give us any information.

On Thursday, Arturo came in. He was another man who the *Washington Post* had written a large article about, picture and all. He was an older man who had spinal arthritis, was a photographer, and always with problems. We had a very fat file on him explaining all the services that had been given to him, but what he really wanted was to work. Even after a year of English classes, he could not learn. This was too difficult, so the Department of Vocational Rehabilitation (DVR) picked up his case and was trying to help him look for some type of employment.

Today, Arturo told me that while he was at the DVR office on Tuesday, someone stole everything in his apartment, at least everything significant. He had a lot of good camera equipment, and it was all gone now. He said since his roommate moved out, he thought that it could have been him, or it could be the gang of twelve who have been robbing houses. I helped him make a police report because he had the names of everyone in the group.

Arturo said he always had everything under lock and key—even the bedroom door—but they broke through the window this time. He went to the landlord for change of locks, and they wouldn't do anything. Arturo told me he was so depressed and just wanted to move away from this area because he was constantly being threatened even by Riko who was accusing him of being communist. They fought out in front of the office one day after the front-page story came out in the *Washington Post* about him.

I had been told that the next story to come out of the *Washington Post* would be about Freddy again. Freddy came in today and said Carmen had three men after him who were going to hang him and kill him. So he did not want trouble and had taken everything out of the apartment, except for his cooking utensils, and said he had his pistol with him just in case. I advised him that this could cause a big problem if he used his pistol, and as I was talking, he pulled out a large blade and showed it to office staff there.

"Freddy, put that away right now!" I said, and he did.

We often had to call the police, and I believe that was one of the times. Translation for the police and ambulance staff was very common these days.

All he wanted at this time was a letter from our office reporting the threats of Carmen's friends, so I wrote one for him. Of course, the police knew both characters and try to avoid them, and that is a fact.

One day, Carmen was so demanding that she asked us to put her in an institution of any sort (she admitted she was mentally ill). We said okay, so we called the police department. An officer came in plain clothes, and she started intimidating him saying she needed a place to live right now! The officer asked her if she wanted to go to jail. She quieted down and said, "No, thank you," so he left. I don't know if I should laugh or cry at these stories now that I read this almost forty years later.

The clients told me that, in their country, they could be thrown in jail for having a Bible. They said that they had to leave their children and all their belongings behind. Many needed a letter from relatives in the United States stating that they would sponsor them. Trying to be a do-gooder, I wanted to place a family in housing that had five children. The parents seemed sincere enough, and the children were very needy.

University Park Church of the Brethren had a house next door that was not being used, so I asked if we could house the family there, and they said yes. Everyone got busy cleaning up the house and appliances, putting in new used furniture, and getting it ready. The family was very appreciative. We invited them to church, but they really could not understand English, so one Sunday, our wonderful Rev. Phillip K. Bradley asked if I wanted to read the Scripture lesson in Spanish. I did this, and it was a flop for two reasons. First, it bored the congregation since they did not understand Spanish, and second, the family became upset because they thought I was singling them out in front of everyone and that the Scripture was specifically meant to pertain to them. They did not come to church anymore after that.

This same family decided they wanted to get their own apartment. With help, we looked for a place in Wheaton, Maryland. They were so happy, and I was happy to find a permanent place for them. They lived there, and the kids went to school. But the downside was that the apartment manager would call me time after time to ask me to ask them to stop killing the pigeons and stop putting the guts down the kitchen sink as there were no garbage disposals at that time. I talked to the family, but they would not stop.

One day, I went over to the apartment to talk to them. As I went in, I noticed that they had a large coat closet. They asked if I wanted to see their "altar," which they would not normally show to just anyone. They said that this was where they offer their sacrifices. They told me this was their religion, called *Santeria*, and that it was a "good religion," but that they did make sacrifices, and that was why there were pigeon guts in the sink—they did not have anything else handy to sacrifice. It was an amazing altar, with plants and statues and incense and candles. I did not know what to think.

One evening, I was listening to a talk show on the radio about religions and cults of the world. I decided to call in. I asked the woman, "What do you know about this *Santeria* religion? Is it real?"

I will never forget her answer. "If you believe it is real, it is real. If you don't believe it is real, it's not." I guess, one could apply that philosophy to a lot of things in life.

I learned that Mr. Jimenez was a very important *santero* (like a witch doctor) in the community and dangerous to some who knew him. This was a religion that had emigrated from Africa and, in Cuba, there was an intensive following.

They explained to me that *Santeria* (at that time), was used primarily for dealing with personal crisis, spiritual, and emotional problems. It appeared to me to be like their own "mental health system" that was highly sensitive to their client's needs. They told me that these beliefs were sometimes referred to as voodoo or witchcraft, and it did not necessarily denote psychological disturbance. I guess such beliefs must be understood within their cultural context.

Those who become members of the cult receive necklaces with specifically colored beads denoting the god or goddess who is assigned as their protector. Many Cubans wear tattoos and beads corresponding to their protector. Mr. Jimenez gave me a yellow and green beaded necklace and told me that if I did not like someone and wanted to "scare" them, just to wear that necklace. I never did find out what it signified!

The tradition said that on December 4, young children are taken from their home, and their blood is drained and their hearts removed and offered to the gods. I was told that from December 3 through December 5, children were kept inside their homes to protect them from being sacrificed. Mr. Jimenez assured me that this was *not* done and that they were sacrificing pigeons instead. That was when the apartment manager would call me.

Then the Montgomery County Executive office called me to ask if I would work with the Refugee Services Program at a much better pay, which I could not turn down. I went to work for the county Refugee Resettlement Program and Cuban/Haitian Entrant program. Through this program, I had the opportunity to serve refugees from Vietnam, Cambodia, Thailand, Laos, Russia, Afghanistan, Iran, and Ethiopia, among others. My days working exclusively with the Cuban entrants, or *Marielitos*, were ending.

The world will change when our children
and women are educated. They will have less
children, and they will raise better families.
When they raise more educated children,
then disease and poverty levels decrease,
and the community and villages change.
(Maggie Doyne, American philanthropist)

CHAPTER 3

Refugee Services in America

I was standing in front of a small classroom of refugees—two from Ethiopia, three from Vietnam, two from Cambodia, and three from Iran. This was a very diverse group, and I was there to teach them how to find a job. They were all newly arrived within the past six to twelve months. They all looked eagerly at me and tried to speak through their broken English. They tried so hard to understand me, and I them. The Iranians were the easiest to talk to because somewhere along the way, they had learned a little bit of English. The Russian refugees told me that they were all "engineers," which, to them, meant anything from a street cleaner to an architect.

I used as many visuals as possible. I brought in employers to talk to them about what they look for in an employee and what to say in an interview. We practiced questions and answers. The clients used what English they knew to ask questions, and they seemed to appreciate the information. The resettlement process included helping the refugees apply for benefits set aside for refugees, which they could receive until they found a job but no longer than eighteen months at that time. The time frame gave them time to settle in and provided an incentive to have their job within the eighteen months.

I had just had my first baby boy back then. Amazingly, a Laotian man and a Japanese father both offered their newborn daughters to me as a wife for my firstborn son when they were old enough. The thought of an arranged marriage is very strange when not belonging to that culture, but it was an honor to know that they thought highly of our family!

Another Vietnamese girl that worked in my office was going to have surgery and wanted to have blood on hand at the hospital in case it was needed. She wanted MY blood reserved, and I asked, "Why mine?"

She said, "Because I know it would be safe, plus, I would like to have whiter skin like yours!" She often came to the office with white makeup on her face that looked rather unnatural. And here, I wanted to have tanned skin like hers!

The refugees told me about the camps that they had lived in for months, and sometimes years, while they were waiting for a sponsor in the United States. This was the saddest part—the children were not able to attend a regular normal school or learn about the outside world. All they knew was the camp in which they had been born and had lived all their lives.

In early 1979, families were fleeing the crumbling regime of Pol Pot, and the Vietnamese soldiers who had invaded to overthrow it. A Cambodian refugee would have to stay in a refugee camp where they were called "displaced persons." To be considered for admittance to the United States, Cambodians in camps along the border had to have had a close family member living there and then file an immigration petition. Many times, they are denied, and this was so discouraging!

A refugee, according to the United States Immigration Service, is "a person who has been forced to leave their country in order to escape war, persecution, or natural disaster." Working with the Refugee Services Program in Montgomery County, Maryland, was an exciting and interesting job. I was able to meet people from all over the world. I specifically was hired to work with Cuban/Haitian entrants (those with Entrant status), but soon, I was interviewing refugees from all over the world.

Most refugees did not speak English, but many came with a translator, and the goal was to help them with the resettlement process. More than anything, they wanted a job, and they wanted to learn English, so this was set up first in that order. I taught the Job Club which taught job search and job retention skills to the refugees. I produced a film on helping refugees get a job and was able to speak to different audiences about the program that we offered.

I was impressed at the level of skill that each person brought. Looking at the women from Iran and Afghanistan amazed me, and I could see that they were strong women in contrast to the "oppressed women" that we had heard of so often. Some were dressed in traditional clothing and others were not. I never found out the determining factor on that.

During this period, I was also asked to be the refugee resettlement coordinator for the Church of the Brethren. This was an exciting position as I traveled throughout Maryland, Delaware, and Virginia, talking to congregations of churches on how and why they should sponsor a refugee. It was interesting to see each different congregation's perspective on sponsoring a refugee. I naively thought that any church-going person, calling themselves a Christian, would agree that it would be important to sponsor a refugee, since this is Bible scripture and something that we are called to do according to what is written in the book of Matthew. I was surprised to find, however, that people are either *afraid* or *threatened* of "strangers" coming into this country. Unbelievably, some were afraid that the refugee would take away their job, or that they would hurt them in some way. This was surprising for me because, in my work with refugees for the past forty years, I have never met one to do any harm or take away a job from the average American.

We, as Christians, are to clothe the naked, feed the hungry, and welcome the stranger into our homes—at least that is what I had been taught as a Christian, but now, I am finding that not all Christians live by that. For the most part, the churches welcomed me and gave me time to make a presentation about why it is important to help our "neighbors," to state my case, and to educate the congregation about the process of refugee resettlement. There were wonderful churches concerned enough to agree to help an individual or family start a new life in the United States, where they could feel safe and be able to have the dignity to earn a living for themselves and their families. I believe that those people and congregations who sponsor refugees will be doubly blessed, or should I say, "blessed sevenfold."

During this time, our church sponsored two Ethiopian/Eritrean refugees. Both were wonderful individuals, but both followed different paths. One had a very difficult time adjusting to the culture and deeply missed his family and his homeland. There had been death and starvation in his country, but he always told me that he wanted to go home so badly. He was thin but had a wonderful smile. The congregation tried hard to help him adjust to the American culture, but he did not assimilate very well, and he ended up committing suicide several years later—and then I knew he had finally gone "home" where he was at peace.

The other refugee from Eretria lived in our church house next to the church and, eventually, became employed and then married. He was very successful and valued the relationship that we had together. He considered the church his new family and was grateful that we had taken the initiative to sponsor him and had rescued him from a horrible situation.

One of the Cambodian refugees that I worked with told me that of the approximately one hundred relatives that he had in Cambodia, eighty-six had been killed during the war. He told me of the years that he spent in refugee camps before being chosen and sponsored to come to the United States. I could tell the trauma was still lingering, but he was able to find a good job with the State of Maryland that allowed him to help other Cambodian refugees like himself.

He also explained to me how it felt as a child to *starve* or to go hungry for days on end. He said, "You will never understand the strength of hunger pains when there is no food to put in the stomach." Sometimes, all they had to eat was a piece of bread and yet that was shared with the other children. He said he could not express enough the sharp pain of hunger! He said, "It hurt to move, and we became dehydrated. It was so hard to swallow, and we were so weak." All through our lives, one will hear the comment, "I'm starving" or

"I am so hungry," but the average American will never feel what he did because we have never gone without any food for days at a time, and we have never experienced the hunger pains that seem to tear our stomachs apart as he mentioned. But I could empathize with him.

I worked with a family from Afghanistan who had three children. They were wonderful people, and they had no furniture, so I was able to arrange to have beds donated to their home as well as a table to eat on. They were forever grateful and surprised at the generosity of the American people.

I worked with many of the Vietnamese, Cambodian, and Laotian refugees, all of which wanted to learn English right away and begin working. They told me of the difficulties in making their way to the United States. I began to learn my numbers in Vietnamese and began to love the food that was so new to me.

One Laotian woman, Nuanne, told me the story of her entry into the United States. "I was twenty-two years old and had two children, and my husband had died. My parents had escaped the incoming communist invasion and had fled for their own safety. They initially were hiding in the countryside for one year but were caught and taken to the refugee camp called the NaPho Camp in Thailand. They did not want to go to the camp initially. We decided to join them because I was alone, with no husband and two children, and what else was I supposed to do? I wanted to be with my parents and my brother!"

Nuanne described the NaPho camp as being inside fences with houses that were built out of bamboo and wood. Young children could go to school for free that was developed by a nonprofit organization, but she said, as an older adult, she had to pay to gain any education. She remembers the camp being overcrowded, and there was not enough food to eat. She said they were not allowed to leave for over six years until they were sponsored.

Her brother and sister also had joined their parents, so at least, the family was together. She said she lived in that camp from 1982 to 1988, and then they were sponsored by another brother who lived in the United States. After living in the NaPho camp for over six years, they were taken to the Philippines where they waited for six months before being taken to the United States in 1988. Once in the United States, they joined her brother and began the resettlement process.

Nuanne said that they were so happy and felt so fortunate to be able to have had the opportunity to immigrate to the United States. Once here, she was able to take care of the children while her brother and sister-in-law worked. She said she took English classes for a while and found it very difficult to concentrate and to learn. Then she married and had two more children, and after four years raising her children, went to work in a seafood company in Pennsylvania.

When have we ever experienced the feeling of helplessness, poverty, starvation, war, and homelessness? This is what others are experiencing every day in many other countries. They are *desperate* for a sponsor, and they pray every day that someone will be kind enough to take them in, whether it is a country, a church, or an individual. Just imagine how it must be like to be completely at the mercy of someone else that you may not even know.

The incredible ending to this story is that this woman is the mother of my now daughter-in-law who married my second son in 2017. Nuanne's wonderful family and children have totally adapted to the American society, and her children are successfully employed and raising their own families. This story could not have ended any better!

There are many things that can only be seen through eyes that have cried. (Oscar Romero)

CHAPTER 4

Helping Our Own

I had been working with refugees and entrants for the past nine years, and so I thought a change would be good and thought about working with the general public through Emergency Services. Our agency was going through budget cuts through the Department of Health and Human Services, and during the Christmas holidays, the director gave us all a coffee cup without a handle on it, saying it was "because of all the budget cuts," which made light of the situation. They needed extra help with the Welfare Reform Back to Work, Project Independence Program which was an initiative to help women on public assistance become self-sufficient through employment and training programs. We worked hard in interviewing and referring (mostly) women to the local community college and jobs that would teach a trade for the women to eventually get off public assistance.

One of the arguments that I always hear from people is, "we should be helping 'our own' before we help others from outside the country!" I say, help those who God presents to us in our lives, in our communities, in our countries, and overseas. We help those who we see in need. Can we help everyone? No, but helping one person or one family, working side by side "one person at a time does it all," as Andy Murray wrote in his song "One Person at a Time" (*Keep on Passing On,* music and lyrics written by Andy Murray, arrangements by Terry Murray. Mediaworks International, Nashville, TN, Murray Music Company, 1998.) "What can one person do is a very good question, if you don't do nothing at all. But if each one would work side by side with one another, the work gets multiplied. Figure it out without a doubt. One person at a time does it all."

I have been very discouraged at the dependence on public assistance that I have seen throughout my work through the Department of Social Services, where I worked for sixteen years. Yes, it is good to help those temporarily who may be going through hard times, and I realize that everyone's situation is different. But as I began to work in the Emergency Services Department, I found that so many of the clients seeking help with electricity bills, food, housing, and burial assistance were hopelessly poor and discouraged as to any hope of getting ahead in America. Although some were first-time applicants for emergency assistance, I saw many more who were lifelong recipients of assistance. It was sad because they, themselves, seemed to have no hope of advancement in their communities.

On the other hand, the immigrant in the communities were low income, but nonetheless, able to save their money and crawl out of poverty through hard work and determination. I did not see many refugees seeking emergency assistance, and many refused handouts if offered. On the other hand, there were many American citizens who were very demanding. Many of the American citizen clients welcomed the opportunity to go back to school and study and find a job, but it was very challenging, to say the least. Most of the individuals that were on welfare at the time were very demanding, and they let it be known. I saw many women whose mothers had brought them up on Public Assistance, and they did not know a different life. They assumed this *was* life. Did they want better? Yes, usually, but they did not know how to get there. They did not know how to apply to go to college when they had no money, and many of them did not have that vision of furthering their education. So began the years of welfare reform.

I consider myself "liberal" and one who cares deeply, but I was grateful for this new welfare reform policy. Soon, there were time limits on welfare, and all recipients had to be in some kind of "welfare to work" program for a certain number of hours per week in order to receive their benefits, or they had to prove they were disabled. What we soon found out by expecting the women to work part time or go to school part time was that the government was now paying a large bill for childcare for their children. And who was to say that the children were better off with a babysitter than with their own mother? Who provides better care? Paying for two to three children in day care while a mother studies or works for minimum wage is good, but in reality, the mother did not want this to be permanent because if she actually made enough money to get off of welfare, then she would lose all of her health insurance (Medicaid) for herself and all of her children and her food stamps, and then what would she do? Plus, how could a single parent earn a living on minimum wage? She could never afford this.

And why weren't the fathers around? It was because a woman could not get welfare, Medicaid, or food stamps if married, with an able-bodied man in the house working, or if the father of the baby did live in the house, it likely meant fraud. That would put them over income for the Medicaid, and they needed the Medicaid, so therefore, the parents would NOT get married in order to keep the benefits. This has caused an avalanche of dependency on the system.

I worked with Americans through Emergency Services for one year, helping with gas and electric bills and housing emergency funds. I worked in public housing units and helped start a program of self-sufficiency and learned what it meant to be a "privileged" white woman. Most white people have privileges that they do not even realize they have or will acknowledge. I saw that there were rarely any immigrants asking for emergency services, just long-term welfare recipients who could not live on that small amount of assistance anyway.

Yes, the "Americans" were a select and special group of individuals. I noticed there were men sitting on their porches during the day and children all around. I talked to some of the men, and they said they did not have anything to do (I cannot confirm or deny that drugs and alcohol played a part in this way of R&R), but they said they needed something to do. So I said, "Let's start a men's support group!"

The men who I saw sitting on their porches were laid back and seemed to be a permanent fixture. They were friends with the neighbors and watched the children as they played outside. They told jokes and seemed to be there for each other—maybe just as a true "community" should be like. They understood each other and helped each other. I asked two of the most motivated men to go out and recruit five or six other men to come to our new group. They seemed to welcome the idea, and soon, we had our own men's group in the public housing development. I found a group leader and told them that the first meeting date would be on Tuesday morning. I told them pizza and drinks would be provided at the meeting, and they were so excited that they all came! Of course, they were expecting pizza and beer but soon straightened that out, that we would not be providing beer but providing education, employment resources, and just plain sharing on how to improve their quality of life. I later learned that group continued for several years.

One man there wanted me to tell his story. He also wanted me to use his name because he felt that, since he was now in hospice, at least he could perhaps leave some kind of legacy in his life.

Andrew had just gotten out of jail. He is now fifty-six years old, with a bald, shaved head and neat clean blue jeans and a sports shirt on. I've known him for years as he has come in faithfully to talk to someone about his horrific life and the emotional and health issues that face him today as a result of child abuse and drug and alcohol abuse as a youth and young man. He valued his therapy, and even his wife would tell him to "go talk to your therapist" whenever they would get into fights. He is highly depressed, often with suicidal thoughts, and talked of nightmares of blood, fires, and of dead people. He could not understand why he was tormented by these things.

One day, he told me that he was entering hospice, that all of his health problems had finally taken over his body, and this time, he had been told to prepare himself for comfort in the unknown remaining time of his life. This is different for him because it had always been that *he* wanted to die or that *he* would be committing suicide. Over the years, he knew to assure me that he would not actually kill himself, although he thought about it all the time. Now, it is different. He was being told that he might be dying, and not by his choice.

I said to him, "You have had such an incredible life of hardship. Perhaps, you could tell others your story." And this was when he told me that he wished everyone would know how hard it was for him, and why he turned out the way he did.

He said, "I have been angry all of my life, and I had no one who understood me or who would stand up for me. I have always been so angry!" He had been raised by his grandmother after his alcoholic mother was killed in a car accident. He did not know who his father was.

Andrew wanted me to tell his story, a story of abuse as a child and of beatings, rape, poverty, alcoholism, bullying, domestic violence, and drug addiction. He told me that he had a long history of jail time, and that there was a reason for it. When I first met him, he said he would never go back to jail; he would die first. However, he was returning from a recent stint and smiled as he told me that, as an older inmate, he was more respected and looked up to, and that the other inmates had nicknamed him Old Triple G because he was the oldest one in there. He said that as long as you weren't a child abuser, you could get along. He said, of all the crimes, he could not tolerate men who abused children. This was because of his own abuse as a child. I have heard this from many men that I have worked with.

He said the worst thing about being in jail was that he could not call home to talk to his two children. His common-law wife would not allow them to talk to him in prison, and he said he could not write a letter, or they would put him in the hole. He said this was the worst thing about being in jail.

What was his life like, and how did he get to where he was today? Andrew was born with fetal alcohol syndrome as his mother was an avid alcoholic. In addition to this, according to his relatives, his mother would give him alcohol in his bottle as a way to keep him quiet. Although highly poisonous to a baby, his family told him that this was his mother's way of sedating him. According to his relatives, he was told that he had seizures and sleep problems in infancy. Growing up, he had poor physical coordination, hyperactivity, learning disabilities, severe behavior problems, low IQ, and language delays. He had problems with daily living, reasoning, and judgment. He said he was always fighting and misbehaving, and he said he felt *out of control.*

Andrew stated that the hardest thing for him was being all alone in his life. He said that if it were not for his grandmother, he would have been in a foster home because his mother was an alcoholic and could not care for him. His mother later died from a car accident after drinking and driving, something that hurt Andrew emotionally. He had always grieved for a mother to love him and care for him, and now he had no mother at all. He always kept her in his heart.

He said he felt the need to protect his little sister and a younger brother. Unfortunately, he had watched his baby sister get raped by his mom's boyfriend. He said he could not tell his mother because she was always too drunk to listen to him. He said, "She never listened to anyone anyway." When his mother died, he remembers the one time he cried. He was at his great-grandfather's house and had two cousins with him when he heard the knock on the door. He saw the police and heard them tell his uncle that his mother was dead. I later listened to Andrew talk about how much he longed for his mother and how much he had longed for her even before she had died, but she was just not available to him.

When he was nine years old, he had three cousins who lured him into the woods, saying they wanted to play. "They pulled my pants down and raped me," Andrew said. "This is why I do not like child molesters. I was beaten all my life because of my bad behavior that I could not seem to control. When I was about thirteen years old, my aunt put me in hot water in the bathtub, and I was severely burned. When I could not learn my math and times tables, my hands would be beaten with a paddle. It was so hard to learn. I saw my first dead person when I was sixteen years old. I've seen a lot of dead things, I've seen a lot of killings, and I even got shot once and almost lost my finger. I see things. It will be at the corner of my eyes. But there is nothing there."

"When I was a kid, we had a two-story warehouse that had a brand-new bathroom. That was exciting because we used to use outdoor plumbing. We were all sitting outside this building, and we saw a woman ghost standing at the window. Another night, my uncle's girlfriend saw a woman ghost standing over us. She had a light-blue dress on, and I know she was my mom watching over us. Ever since then, I have been seeing things. This was when I was about eighteen years old."

Andrew said he did not have anyone to play with when he was little. He said he had the little green army men and pigs and tractors to play with. At Christmas, they all got stockings with candy and oranges and apples and grapefruit in it. He remembers having a nice Christmas. This was at a time when his mother lived down the street, and his brother and sister were there too.

He said he remembers that he would run back and forth from his grandmother's house to other neighbors' houses. He remembers being the smallest kid around the neighborhood, and he would want to hang out with someone, but there were only grown people. The grown people would tell him that if he wanted to hang around with them, he would have to drink and smoke with them. This was when he began drinking, smoking, and using drugs.

When he was twelve years old, he was in a special home for boys and then later transferred to a detention center for boys. He said, "I was just so angry, and I was always fighting, getting beaten up, and getting in trouble in school. I had to learn to fight. I would take weapons to school, and one time, a boy took a knife to school, and I took it from him and then I was the one who got locked up for it! People would call me Hound Dog or Puppy Dog because I was always frowning in school."

Andrew said that school was difficult for him. He said, from eighth grade on, he sat in the principal's office and did his class-work. "They did not want me to go to class because they said I was a bad influence on my teacher. I even slept with a teacher. She would always ask me, 'Can you come to my house and clean up my dirty underwear?'" He said he was only fourteen or fifteen, and the rela-tionship went on for about two years. He did not mind, and who was going to believe him anyway? He said he was doing many deviant sexual things he knew he should not have been doing, but at the time, he did not care. He said he would have sex in school behind the auditorium curtain. He said he would show his private parts and look up the girls' dresses. But he said no one really cared about him.

Andrew reported that he had been in mental institutions about five or six times, mostly for suicidal thoughts. He said he tried to commit suicide three times—once he cut his wrist, once he tried to hang himself in a tree, and then he tried to overdose on his medications.

Andrew said, "I hung around mostly with white guys and girls even though I was black because I couldn't seem to get along with dark-skinned guys. They would always try to get me to fight them. I felt like there was a discrimination just among the black, and I am black! The black kids would spit on me!"

When he was in jail, he said the men would also spit on him, but he said he did not fight because he knew spitting in jail was a felony. One day, he said he only had two days left in jail, and the men were spitting on him, but he did not fight. He said that was one time when he was able to refrain, but it was so hard to do so because he had learned to be a fighter.

Andrew stated that his wife is Indian, lighter-skinned then he is, and his grandfather was Indian, about six feet tall. He would say to people, "I am going to make you famous. I was going to put them in an obituary." He said he would say, "Hell's coming with me" or "I'll be your Huckleberry" when he would get in fights, which meant "I'll be that person you'll want to fight. I would fight for my friends because they couldn't fight."

Today, Andrew has a common-law wife that he is now separated from after she found out that he had returned to using drugs again. He has two boys that he loves dearly. One of his boys is autistic, and he has spent his life caring for that boy, lifting him onto the bus every day, changing him, caring for his most essential needs. All of this lifting caused several back problems that required surgery later, part of the pain that Andrew carries with him today.

Andrew has always had suicidal thoughts but says that he chose to live for his two boys. He said he lived through hell to get to where he is today. His younger son also is at risk because of the drugs and alcohol in the public housing neighborhood that he lives in, but

Andrew loves him and tries to be a better father to them than what he had, which was no father.

He said, "I took care of my sons the way they should have been taken care of. I love them. I was lucky to be with them for fifteen years, before my wife made me leave. This is what hurts the most. I cannot be with them now. She called my probation office, and my probation officer said I had to go in and do a urine test. I did not have anyone to take me to do the urine test, so my wife got mad, and she called the police. I got smart with the police officer because I did not want to put my hands behind my back. Then they found that I had drugs and a pipe in my pocket. And that is why I am where I am today."

The officer who took him to the station reminded him of an earlier time many years ago, when a cop broke his leg with a night stick. He said he had to wear a cast for six months. His sister had wanted him out of her house, and since he would not leave, the police came and were trying to get him out of the house and were going to bust open the window. Andrew said he got into a tussle with the officer and was wrestling with the him while kids in the neighborhood stood around taking pictures. The officer ended up breaking his leg with his night stick.

Andrew stated that he always had dreams and nightmares of dead people, setting fire onto things. His nightmares are not as severe today as they used to be. He said he talks and yells in his sleep. He remembers his dreams, and he said that each time he was in prison, he would have to see a therapist or doctor because of his nightmares and thoughts of hurting people and hurting himself.

In the end, Andrew told me, he didn't have a chance. He knows that he was product of his surroundings, of his upbringing, of his lot in life. He said he now is facing his mortality and would like to leave in peace, which is why we spoke of his destiny during his remaining session and God's never-ending love for him. Was I supposed to do this as a social worker? I don't hesitate to do so when I see the open door into a man or woman's heart, who is longing for something to bring them peace. I only hope that I was able to do so in time for this one man's life.

This was the story of a black American male, but it could have been anyone's story. Anyone who grows up in a disadvantaged family, full of drugs and alcohol, and abuse are just as serious as those of immigrants who are seeking refuge from violence, death, and destruction in the United States. Everyone has a cross to bear. These stories are common with many that I have talked to and, in comparison, are just as serious as those immigrants who are coming into the United States for a better life. The American citizen also has his/her problems and probably do not take into account that they are lucky enough to have a social security card, a passport, a driver's license, and that they can speak English without thinking about it. Let's face it, there *is* a minority of Americans who are *not* motivated to work like the immigrant—to study, to provide a good life for their family. In August 2019, there was a white supremacist who killed several Hispanics at an El Paso Walmart because he feared that they were taking something from him as an American. Perhaps, he was even afraid that he was going to be "replaced" as the newscaster said. In the same news flash on TV, they said that this American terrorist, on the other hand, was known to be lazy and unmotivated, often playing violent video games. Now, there is something that we, as a nation, have to work on!

BUT the reality of the American often is that children are born every day to drug-addicted and alcoholic mothers. Children are abused all their life by aunts and uncles and societal predators such as teachers and priests. Don't blame the motivated immigrant who is seeking to better their lives though education and employment. We need to blame a system that cannot improve the educational system and fix the drug problem in the United States. It is not the child's fault that they grow up in a broken system; it is our fault for not using compassion and foresight to notice the injustice, the pain, and suffering in the world. How about we step up to make that change for a better world? That does not mean place more guns into the community and increase death-row statistics. It means trying to work with the alcoholic, the drug addict, the children who were not fortunate to be born into an emotionally healthy family. And no, it is not money that will make us healthy; it is the love and compassion that we have for other people. We are all one in this universe. Let us stop hurting each other! *And that is Andrew's message to the world!*

While working at the projects, the department was able to find the staff they needed to continue the program, and I moved on to child welfare, where I, as the *peon*, was sent out to pick up children from their screaming parents, to place into foster care. I only did this for six months because I thought I was beginning to have heart problems from the stress that this created. I do not believe in abusing children or neglecting children, but to rip the children from the parent, to me, was too heartbreaking. I had four children at that point, and I would ask myself, "What makes me any better parent than those parents?" None of us have had any training in parenting. What could we do to support and teach young parents the art of parenting and nonviolence? This is something that needs to be taught in high school or even earlier.

I soon asked to be sent to another program. I wanted to use my Spanish again, and I wanted to work in the school system. I felt the Americans were too hard to work with and the issues too deep. My desire was to work out in the community with all people of all nationalities, and so my next position was to work in the center of an urban community elementary school, with the goal of bringing parents to the school to help their children succeed in their education.

You shall not oppress the resident alien—you
know the heart of an alien for you were aliens in
the land of Egypt. (God, Exodus 23:9 NRSV)

CHAPTER 5

Working with Central Americans

I was sent to help the Linkages to Learning Program develop at
Highland Elementary, Silver Spring, Maryland, along with two
other elementary schools. I worked with staff of the school, the medical providers—nurses, the mental health professionals who would be
working out of the office at the school and the Department of Social
Services to address the needs of the families. This was a wonderful
program.

The University of Maryland did a study on the program to see
if linking comprehensive services to the families right in the community would make a difference. Did "wrap around services" help parents become more connected to their community schools, and did
it help the child to learn and thrive better in this supportive atmo-
sphere? Of course, it did. The outcome measures were very positive.

When I started working at Highland Elementary it was only
about 33 percent Hispanic. When I left the school nine years later, it
was about 68 percent Hispanic. I do not know if it was because we
had mostly all bilingual staff, but we provided whatever resources the
parents needed in order to help them become a part of their child's
education.

We began parenting classes and therapy groups for parents,
developing activities and training that parents wanted. The parents
were often shy about coming to the school in the beginning. But I
had learned through the Peace Corps that if we offered any type of
program that was set up to help their children, the parents would

come because parents would do anything necessary to help their children. We began a Parent's Anonymous group in Spanish and trained the parents to be their own leaders in the group. We offered workshops on several topics of interest. The first workshop requested by parents was, "How to Talk to Your Child About Sex." Well, that grabbed everyone's attention. The therapy groups were developed according to need. We had a support group for parents with ADHD children and learned that we needed a whole lot of help in providing childcare for those children while parents were in the group—as they were highly animated!

We began the *Linkages to the Library* program where we transported children and their parents to the local library during the summer and connected them with volunteers who read to the children. Every week during the summer, we had a bus transport the families to the library and there, volunteers would be sitting in corners all over the library reading to the children. The parents became involved and listened to the stories alongside their children. We taught parents how to use the computers and how to obtain a library card and check out books. Many of the immigrant families were unaware of this excellent resource, not only for the children but for themselves as adults. They were able to access materials that would help them learn English and were able to use the computers to seek employment. The families were given freebees, T-shirts, and other books and giveaways to enhance their motivation.

We developed a retreat for mothers who had never had a break from their children or family and nurtured the mothers at a lodge in western Maryland. This was so popular that, soon, we had a waiting list. We received funding from an outside grant, and with the money, we provided transportation, food, lodging, therapy groups, arts and crafts, and just plain relaxation for the mothers. We paid for childcare so that they could leave town for two nights. This was very difficult for the mothers as many had never had a break from their children and had never been separated from them.

The women were treated like queens. They had their own fancy room with flowered wallpaper and fluffy pillows. They each received a massage and relaxed in the hot tub overlooking the mountains of northern Maryland. They shared their artistic abilities through guided activities and discussed the importance of living in the present and noticing the flowers. The setting was beautiful! The retreat center actually had a real tree growing up right through the middle of the house. The women were able to take hikes, work with clay, and share stories. They sat on the chairs outside and watched the horses on the hillside, and they walked the labyrinth. They loved it and soon looked forward to the women's retreat every spring. We called it the "Mother's Day Retreat" because many of the husbands did not want them to go. We told the husbands that this was a gift to the mother's and that they would benefit from a happier wife in the future!

We matched the men and women who were struggling to learn English with a mentor from the nearby church, which created deep relationships with the immigrants who did not know anyone and was having a difficult time making new friends and practicing the language. Each Wednesday night we matched the parents from Mexico, Central and South America with our friends from the Methodist Church to meet to just talk—talk about anything. It was not a class; it was a "mixer" and relationship-building initiative. One elderly couple was so happy because they had been adopted as the children's grandparents. The children of immigrants were so happy because now they had "grandparents"! Many of the immigrant parents had come to the United States, leaving their families behind, and so their children did not know grandparents. The partnerships and friendships that developed through this program were priceless as the "grandparents" would be called to join the families at holidays, and if there was a family crisis, they often depended on each other for help. It was a benefit to both sides.

I was always available to the parents on a walk-in basis, to provide information and referral and short-term counseling for the parents. One day, a mother of five children from El Salvador came to me in desperation, stating that she had thought about taking her children down to the railroad tracks that morning to kill herself and her children.

She cried as she said, "I cannot take any more abuse by my husband! I think it would be better to die and to take my children with me because he is so evil, and I cannot get away from him! My arm has been broken for the second time, and he will not go away."

This woman had been to the local shelter, and the husband had been in treatment, yet he continued to live in the basement of the home—separated from the family but still there. The domestic violence center, along with a no-contact order helped to remove this man from her home, and through hours of support by the community and therapy provided to her and her children, there was a positive outcome, and she became very involved with the program and the school.

Salvadorans were immigrating to the United States during the 1980s because of a long history of oppression and exploitation as a result of the civil war in their country which, sadly, was partially funded by the United States. Prior to the war, Central Americans came to the United States for economic reasons, but now they were fleeing without any preparation or support—in other words, escaping. I heard someone refer to these immigrants as "displaced persons." Because of this, they seemed to have a much more difficult time adjusting to the new culture. Most immigrants will tell you that they would rather live in their own country, but now, so many are forced to leave for fear for their lives as well as for economic reasons as their towns and countrysides were being destroyed by the war.

Individuals who were coming from a rural area of El Salvador or Guatemala, where there are soft green countrysides and vast spaces, were often thrown into a small apartment, with many other relatives and/or friends, in a noisy, dirty, large city and were experiencing culture shock and despair. Many of these immigrants told me that the worst part was the isolation that they felt. In their towns, the community lived and worked together, worshiped and played together. But they said, "In the United States, everyone keeps their doors shut. The children cannot go out and play, and there is not such a feeling of community." They told me that this was the hardest thing to cope with in the United States. They told me they felt alone, too shy to practice their English with anyone. So they shut themselves into their houses, becoming more and more depressed and isolated. The acculturation process slowed because of the fear of the newness, the fear of being sent back to their country, and the depression that often follows culture shock. They were missing their families and their children. But at the same time, they felt desperate and that there was no other choice. They not only feared for their safety, but they wanted something better for their children.

It is also not easy to learn another language, although many tell me they have taken English classes. So often, when an individual is illiterate in their own language, it is twice as hard to learn a foreign language. I know the difficulty because it took me years to learn the Spanish language well, and I also felt shy in practicing another language.

As immigrants arrived in the United States, most face what we would call poverty, but to the immigrant, a roof over their head and the opportunity to work in the fields or in the chicken plant is a welcome way of surviving, so much better than what they had come from. One woman even told me that she was so surprised when a man offered her a job in the fields of Florida and, at the end of the week, gave her a paycheck! She told me, "I have never in my life earned a paycheck, and on top of that, I do not even have to sell my body in return!" This was the first form of income that she had ever received for her hard work that did not involve sexual favors, and she said, from that day on, she has worked in *real* jobs and has never had to sell herself again in order to survive.

In 1986, the US government granted temporary work permits to the Salvadorans through the Immigration Reform and Control Act of 1986 which enabled Central American refugees to seek employment legally, however, the new law no longer allowed employers to hire immigrants without legal documents. This 1986 law barring employers to hire undocumented aliens was thought to have caused discrimination to many Hispanics as some employers assumed *all* Hispanics are illegal. The educational level, skill level, and English ability also were a barrier to many of those seeking employment, and still is.

The same thing happened to the Guatemalan immigrants, in which there was TPS (Temporary Protected Status) protection and ability for the individuals to legally prove that they were paying taxes on their income and were good "citizens." The TPS program allowed them to work legally and contribute to society in a good way.

Following are three accounts of stories of immigrants coming from Central American countries.

Guadalupe came to the United States in 1985 because of the war and the effects of the economy in El Salvador. There was no other way to support her family which consisted of her mother, two sisters, and two daughters. She said if it were not for the war, she would never have come here. She had only seen her two daughters once in their early years as they were growing up and was grieving for them every single day. Because of the war, everyone was afraid to go out of their houses. Her house was in the city, and there was gunfire every day and soldiers walking the streets. She said she and her family decided it would be best that she make the trip to the United States, find a job, and send money back to El Salvador.

In the earlier years, Guadalupe made only $250 a week in the United States and sent $250 a month back to her country, which supported her whole family. She had to leave her children when they were ages one and seven. Guadalupe came through Mexico by plane and then to Tijuana, where she too hired a coyote (guide) to take her across the border, however, not before she was raped, assaulted, and robbed while crossing. For this reason, she did not send for her children—it was too dangerous.

Carlos came to the United States from El Salvador in 1981, soon after the war had just begun. He told me that soldiers were coming into the homes and grabbing any young man that they found. They would take fathers of children, and if there was resistance, they would kill the fathers and, sometimes, the whole family. Animals were being stolen, and houses were being burned. People were fleeing, crossing borders in nearby countries to escape the atrocities of war. Refugee camps were being set up, but the violence continued even in the camps. There seemed to be no safety anywhere. So he and his son decided to immigrate to the United States out of fear for their lives and fear of being recruited as soldiers.

Carlos told me he and his son had taken a plane from El Salvador to Mexico and, from Tijuana, hired a guide to take him across the border. He was robbed several times and feared for his life at the border because people tried to take everything he owned, including his legal documents (birth certificates, etc.). It took six hours to walk across the mountain to San Diego with a group of about six people. He joined his brother who was already in California but had a difficult time finding employment. They lived in California for six years before coming to Maryland where he had heard there was work.

When he arrived in Maryland, he was able to work in the construction business and make enough money to support himself and his son, while sending dollars back home to help the rest of his family. He was able to receive asylum and, later, permanent residency. And today, he is the owner of a construction company that employs ten other people and supports their families here in the United States. This is a story of how the immigrant can benefit our society in more ways than one. His son is now a successful businessman in Washington, DC.

Both Carlos and Guadalupe worked in the United States through the TPS program which expired in June 1994. Guadalupe was able to find an employer to sponsor her, but it took over ten years for the process because in 1989, an American immigration lawyer took thousands of dollars from her without actually processing any paperwork. If he would have done his job, she would have been a legal permanent resident after two years.

During his interview, Carlos spoke of the discrimination that he was experiencing. He said, "At work, the Americans do not like to see Hispanics, and they tell us to go back to our country. They tell us that we are taking all the jobs away from them. But if you think about it, all we are doing is the work that they do not want to do. For example, I have been paid minimum wage to clean their bathrooms and pick crabs on the eastern shore of Maryland. But all of that was a steppingstone to where I am today, a productive member of society."

In the same interview, this man stated that he has had policemen stop him while sitting at a red light in an intersection and interrogated for being a drunk driver. When trying to reason with the policemen in broken English, the police would say, "Here in the United States, you don't speak Spanish. You have to speak English. You shouldn't be here anyway." Carlos stated that he has always been a law-abiding member of the community, has contributed to the economy in the area, and has served this country well. He stated that he feels hurt that he is profiled in this manner.

Carlos's family, in seeking housing, has received rude behavior from many apartment complexes. This manager would very subtly pay no attention to them when they would inquire about an apartment. He stated that, "It makes you feel really bad when the manager purposely picks up the telephone and carries on a long casual conversation right in front of me as she avoids talking to me."

Carlos feels blacks have it worse than the Hispanics do. In the workplace, he says there is a general feeling that blacks are lazy and do not like to work. However, his boss is black and a very good man who works hard. His boss told him once that he had been treated very unfairly until the other employees learned that he was actually the supervisor.

Another Salvadoran couple stated that there is even discrimination in Spanish restaurants. They had walked into a Spanish restaurant before white patrons, and the hostess walked right past them to seat the American couple first.

In speaking with a teenager who has the goal of going to college, she explained, with an accent, that she does not experience much discrimination, but her parents, who have tried but not been able to learn English, do. She says that after fifteen years in the United States, they long to go home soon, even though they have finally acquired their residency.

Most people come to this country with the feeling they are going to be here *temporarily*. They want to save money, build a house, send their children to school, and then return to their country, not necessarily in that order. So often, they meet their husband or wife, have children, and then their children have children, and it becomes harder and harder to leave. They feel it is too risky to leave because they know they will *not be able to return* to *visit* their children and grandchildren. I have heard from many immigrants that they would like to return to their country, but *not* if they will never be able to see their families again in the United States. Ability to come and go legally, would be an answer to this problem because applying "the right way" as it is today may take years, and some people do not have years—especially if fleeing their country due to death threats and natural disasters.

Coming across the border, *Rosa* (El Salvador) said she saw EVERYTHING. She told me that she did not know where she was going but that she had to escape the violence in her town. The gangs were taking over. She could not walk down the street without being threatened. She was hypervigilant and watching every person that came near her or lurked around the corner. She was deathly afraid of everything and could not trust anyone. She trembled as she spoke about the assaults that she experienced throughout her life. She could not bear to continue this lifestyle and decided that she had to leave.

As she traveled north, she did not know what her future would bring. She said she would travel for a while and then wash dishes in some restaurant in order to eat and pay bus fare. She was alone and did not know what the future held for her. She said that when she neared the border, she met other women who were also fleeing their country. Together, they cried and promised that they would stick together for safety purposes.

As the group came closer to the border, she witnessed a drug cartel taking two women away, and she does not know what happened to them but could only guess. She said they took the most beautiful and youngest girls. She feared for her own safety but said that, perhaps, they did not take her because she was older and less attractive. She saw a man assaulted and robbed, and they took him away too.

She said she did not realize that she was in great danger. She said she walked so much in the middle of the dessert full of snakes, and she was so afraid of snakes. She did not have a guide to help her, and what she witnessed horrified her. She saw total families waiting by the river to cross. She cried so much because she said she had never seen so many bad people. She saw desperate people who were trying to reach safety from the violence and murder in their country, but they had to experience more violence in order to escape. She said that what she had heard was that there was safety in the United States.

She said that once she crossed the river, they all stayed in one little house, and that same day, ICE (Immigration) found them. She felt much safer after they were discovered and under ICE custody. Right before they were discovered, there were men asking for money from them for helping them cross the river. She said she did not have any money, and just then, United States ICE showed up. She said that she stood there frozen.

Along the way, one of the women who she had been travelling with suddenly disappeared, and she carries with her great guilt because they had sworn they would stick together, but she does not know what happened to her. Did she wander off, or was she kidnapped? Rosa continues to feel guilt for not being able to keep her promise to stick together.

She said they had worn the same dirty clothes for days, and she had not eaten but also did not have any appetite. She had come all alone because she was running for her life. She feels that she lives with that same fear that she had for her life in El Salvador every single day and knows that she needs counseling to help with symptoms of severe post-traumatic stress disorder. She said that her fear of having to return to El Salvador is almost as big as her fear of being killed in El Salvador.

Today, there are gangs in El Salvador that are practically running the country. They will look for you and find you easily because they talk to each other between towns and cities. Different clients have explained that the *Mara Salvatrucha* "own" different zones in the city, and they require identification from individuals who want to go from one zone to another. I have been told that they request identification because one must "belong" to the zone in order to enter and then, sometimes, they ask for a fee in order to leave. I'm told that if you are not from that zone, they will take everything you have, rob you, and can even kill you. And if you get away without paying certain fees, they can locate you within twenty-four hours because of communication between gang members. It is very hard to escape them.

It is well known from the people that I spoke to that the *Mara Salvatrucha 18* is controlling the zones, using extortion and threats to murder in order to control the government politicians and police. Many of the women who are attacked and held by the gang members and raped are not able to make reports to the police because of retaliation. According to endless accounts of stories of those seeking asylum, there is no real protection in the country. The country is full of corruption, not only in El Salvador, but in Honduras, Guatemala, Mexico, and other neighboring countries. I am told that the drug cartels are worse in Mexico.

According to a *Washington Post* article in 2016, Salvadoran gangs are descendants of gangs formed in Los Angeles in the 1980s by immigrants who fled their country's civil war. Many of their leaders were eventually deported back to El Salvador, and this was when they began to control the neighborhoods. Their members extort residents, kill, kidnap, rape, and serve as sentries against rival cliques. The gangs and experts who study them estimate their active ranks at 70,000 people, not including the tens of thousands behind bars.

Almost all applicants for asylum that I have interviewed are fleeing their country because someone in their family has been threatened. Many times, a gang has murdered a family member and has threatened to murder more. Each circumstance is unique, and the immigrants are traumatized and seeking refuge and safety for themselves and their children.

Do we need to secure the borders from the violent offenders? Yes, we do, but we have also created the problem as offenders from the United States are sent back to their country and then are coerced into joining one of the gangs. If we keep the offenders in the United States, then it is also costly to give them room and board in our prisons. If we send them back to be "punished" in their own countries, then many times, they end up on the streets, robbing and injuring others. How can this be resolved? I really do not have the answer, except that we cannot turn our backs on the victims, and we need to be proactive in controlling the crime and poverty when we can. And since we *are* the United States, I am sure we can do something. By doing nothing, we are doing something.

When the church hears the cry of the oppressed,
it cannot but denounce the social structures
that give rise to and perpetuate the misery
from which the cry arises. (Oscar Romero)

CHAPTER 6

Walking with the Church
Leaders, El Salvador

(January 23–February 2, 1992)

In 1992, I was asked to go to El Salvador with my church during the last week of the war in El Salvador. We were to accompany church leaders there and stand with them during possible conflict that week. Wow, this was so exciting. Even though I had a newborn at home, I welcomed the chance for a trip to Central America and to represent the Church of the Brethren and the National Council of Churches. So I accepted, although I felt quite unqualified to talk to anyone. We were able to meet representatives of the *Sandinistas*, government officials, and other church leaders from different parts of the world about political events of that time. But I went and felt most at home with the country people. I saw an orphanage outside of the city, of children who had been abandoned by the war. There were signs of cracks throughout San Salvador where the earthquake had hit. I shared my Brethren Peace Fellowship button with a Sandinista boy and told him what it stood for. One never knows what that might have meant to that young soldier.

We arrived in San Salvador about 2:00 p.m. the first day and were driven out to the *Casa del Huespedes* by an American guide and a Salvadoran host. I did not think we would make it the way they were driving up the mountain. There were military all along the road, with rifles pointing up the mountain. I asked what they were doing, and they jokingly said they were hunting for their supper.

I was travelling with representatives from all over the world, who were representing the World Council of Churches. This trip was in response to the need for representatives to form a chain of solidarity of the National Council of Churches in El Salvador (CNI) and to "walk with" church leaders who had continued to receive death threats in their country. Our stay included meeting with the Human Rights Commission, several conventions, government offices, and the National Debate Committee. This was a very rich experience. I met a fellow Church of the Brethren member, a representative from the United Church of Christ, and a woman from Germany representing the World Council of Churches. The National Council of Churches in El Salvador (CNI) had formed the group in order to try to strengthen their churches to rebuild the country after years of war. The peace accords were signed January 16, 1992, and the cease-fire was on January 17, 1992. Before we had arrived, the CNI had received a letter listing eleven leaders by name, to tell them that they would be killed if they did not leave the country within seventy-two hours.

The day we arrived was the most frightening one of my trips. The wife of one of the church leaders had been abducted and injected with a substance that caused her to black out, and so she could not remember anything that happened. She had also been beaten and questioned about her husband who was one of the pastors. She was returned twenty-four hours later, having been beaten, drugged, and forced to reveal the names of the leaders. They warned her that "this was for real," and that they could be killed.

As scared as these people were, they were not going to leave the country. They hoped that because of our presence there, nothing would happen, and nothing did happen. As we left, another team arrived so that there would always be support for the leaders. It was good to know that our presence there may have made a difference in the life of those church leaders.

On the first day, I was getting into a taxi and was stung by a bee. I've been stung before, but this was different. My right forearm became very swollen and red, painful and hard. I did not know what to do. Luckily, one of the reps from the National Council of Churches from California, who had been living in El Salvador for the past five years, happened to be a medical professional and knew what I needed. We went to the pharmacy, and he injected me with adrenalin, gave me Benadryl, and by the next day, the swelling had gone down.

I found out later that he was a volunteer put in charge of the Artificial Limb project in El Salvador. He said they received most of their funds from Jubilee Partners in Georgia! He said they distribute the funds, the factory makes the limbs, and he sees the children and makes sure they get what they need. Sometimes, the children must go to the United States to have surgery. He also does reconstructive face and mouth surgery. All these services are free to the people. His wife was also a social worker and would travel with the kids back and forth to the United States. I talked to him about how it was to bring his own children into a foreign country, and he stated that they had adapted well.

I met another woman who was there on assignment from the Lutheran Church. She told me she did not know much about the politics of the land and did not know the people. She felt it was better that she did not know anything just in case she was captured and drugged like the other Salvadoran woman was.

The next day, we went through a small city, and there were people everywhere. I had never seen a country so crowded. During the twelve years of war, the fighting was generally fought in the countryside, and the people would migrate to the cities to avoid the conflict. On the outskirts of San Salvador, there were new urban areas made up of shacks filled with people, and many of these individuals had no jobs. We were told that there was 40 percent unemployment in El Salvador at that time.

One of the highlights of the week was the trip to Las Minas where we heard stories of village people who had fled El Salvador for Honduras. We were invited into a small wooden house where townspeople met and explained to us what had happened to the people in the town. We listened to the horror stories of the war and the loss that the town and innocent families had experienced.

Next, we were guided up the mountain, which was very difficult, and it was very hot. I could hardly make it, but finally, we reached a clearing where there were dozens of military men and boys with rifles, all looking at us. We were so hot, so we went straight to the river and took our shirts off and got into the water to cool off. It felt so good but was probably not the smartest thing to do as it was the FMLN opposition party who was there. But the men were calm and decent and talked to us of their own frustrations for peace during all this time of war. They spoke of the violence, hatred, and death that the war had created, but they were in front of us telling us that all they wanted was peace, and that this was about to happen that weekend as they waited for the peace accords to be signed!

There were young boys who were in uniform standing around as well as the leaders who had surely taken them from their parents and their families to fight. I asked one man what they planned to do after the war, and he indicated that they would go back to their hometowns and continue farming as he loved. He told me that the people who were fighting there had not been fighting for power but as an *obligation* and *duty* to help the communities and the people. Now, he said their duty was finished, and they could return to what they were doing before the war. I wanted to give them a "peace offering" and something to remember, so I took the Brethren Peace Fellowship pin that I had with me, with a cross and a dove, and pinned it on one of the officers.

Back in Chalatenango, everyone in the streets was excited, singing and happy because the peace accords had been signed, and a big fiesta was planned for the day of the cease-fire. When we asked people if the war was truly over, they said, "We hope, we really hope." The Salvadoran army was there but very quiet. We spoke with representatives of one army group, and they told us they, too, were hopeful. We asked why they were still there in uniform, with guns, and they said they were waiting for orders to disband—but it would still take about nine months to completely disband. We saw children with them—a thirteen-year-old, in uniform with guns. As the war was twelve years old at that time, he must have known nothing but war all his life.

We visited a pueblo, where twenty-five families were living, which had been destroyed during the war. One building, a childcare center, had been built under the direction of the Lutheran Church. Each villager worked two days a week on the rebuilding project and, the rest of the week, in the fields to support their families. They had a barn with thirty stalls filled with healthy looking pigs. A German missionary came to provide health care to the people. Many wonderful volunteers, from many places and many countries, have made the choice in their lives to help these people over time and to rebuild their towns.

The next day, we visited Montepeque and three small *repoblaciones* which were being developed. There, we saw unbelievable poverty in areas with no water or electricity but which did have food, tents, a dentist, and plans for acquiring basic needs before the rainy season in May. People were returning to build their homes. We met a man who had been living in the United States but had returned to El Salvador because he felt the United States was starting to "turn into poverty like El Salvador," and he called it "doomsday" because he said every time he went to the United States, he saw more and more poverty, homelessness, and street people, etc. He said the United States will "fall just like British Columbia."

One of the Salvadoran pastors said he really felt safe with our group, so he said he was tempted to stay with us until the cease-fire which was to happen that week. Another man, Ignacio, went into hiding because of all the death threats he had received.

The earthquake was in 1986, and the United States had provided many funds to help rebuild, but the people told us the money was never seen or used by the people who needed it the most. Many refugees had fled from Rio Sumpul, where 600 people had been slaughtered in 1980. They were now trying to repopulate the area and rebuild the homes.

Another highlight of the trip was to visit the Esperanza y Fe Orphanage which held groups of children orphaned by the war. They seemed to be well looked after. There was a career building where they were teaching the children to sew, make clothing, arts, and crafts, etc. so that they would be able to work a trade when they left there. Many were hoping to find their parents now that the war was ending.

The church had begun this center in 1982, but in 1987, someone had put a bomb into the building, and the whole building collapsed, including the kitchen area, Red Cross, school, dorms, and fence around the area. Now they were attempting to repopulate the elderly and the refugees. Teachers were brought there to teach.

We visited the university where the Jesuit priests and their servants had been massacred. We drove into a beautiful garden and building that was so peaceful. At first, we did not know where we were. It was so clean and pretty! We then went to the pastoral building. We were taken to a very small library where we were shown two graphic notebooks with pictures of the Jesuit priests who were massacred. There was a library with torn Bibles, which the assassins had ripped apart, and pictures of the priests which they had torn from the walls. They had been the most knowledgeable, analytical prophetic minds of the world for the Salvadoran people, and the country was stunned. Seven priests and two women in the barracks had been sleeping, and "someone" came in and shot them in the yard.

At first, everyone thought it was the FMLN who had committed the murders, but later found out it had been their own Salvadoran military. It was discovered that the army had taken their own soldiers who had been in the area that night, put them in the front middle of the combat zone, and then assassinated them shortly after so that there would be no one to admit to the killings. This brought to life the reality of the fact that, every day, people are threatened, in danger, and assassinated.

Threats ceased at least for this week, and church leaders were able to continue with their individual worship programs. One event that they were planning was a large youth retreat. We visited the retreat and could see the leadership ability emerging in the young people as they led worship. The youth will be regarded as playing an important role in church growth and in personal healing after a war. The country was then trying to free itself from its oppression. People were just beginning to be able to express themselves and their faith without fear.

On January 23, 1992, I went to see a friend's family in San Salvador who had six children. Lupe, who lives in the United States, sends money home each month which pays for everyone's food in that family, including her own children who she left so that they could be fed and attend school. She explained that she had also been involved in a student movement in the early '80s and decided to leave for her own safety. The father of her oldest child fled from the army to Guatemala and then disappeared. She then had another fiancé, but he disappeared also.

The house was made of cement block and had a patio outside where much of the cooking was done. The latrine was also outside. Lupe stated that her family's home was destroyed by an earthquake in 1986, and of course, there was no insurance there, and they lost everything. In 1990, they rented a small home across from a command center of the army and were caught in a crossfire for eight solid days. She stated that the smell of the dead was horrible and something she will never forget. They hid under the beds all that time. She talked of the eleven-year-old who could not sleep for weeks because of nightmares. At the time, she was unsure as to whether the cease-fire would be just yet another inevitable failure.

The people of El Salvador were living in danger, and we prayed for the safety of all those involved in the struggle as well as those who were there to help. What would it be like if our church leaders were being threatened in the United States? What would our congregations do? Would we do something, leave, or simply pray for safety? The faith of the people was strong and moving as we witnessed such love and faith at the various church services that we attended. Despite the threats, some stayed, and some left the country. One song that was being sung was "we are still singing, we are still asking, we are still dreaming, we are still hoping, we are still waiting." The sad thing is that almost forty years later, the people are still living in fear.

"When you look into someone else's eyes and you see yourself looking back, then you've reached a higher level of understanding because we are all connected" —Anonymous

CHAPTER 7

Teaching Nonviolence

After working with refugees from several different countries, my husband and I moved to the Eastern Shore of Maryland and Delaware where life was at a slower pace. It took a lot of discernment to come to that decision, but the calling was strong and would not be regretted. Again, I felt like we were in a different world and a different culture altogether.

I began working with an agency in Delaware providing therapy and other social services to the community. The agency asked that I teach the Non-Violence Intervention Program to men batterers both in English and in Spanish. I was sent to Minnesota for the Duluth training and was also trained to work with Hispanic men by the Training Center to Eradicate Masculine Intrafamily Violence (Antonio Ramirez) out of California. I never realized that this job would end up being one of the most rewarding jobs that I would ever have.

I began to get acquainted with the Guatemalan and the Mexican communities in Delaware, where most of the immigrants were working in the poultry plants and the watermelon fields. Most Americans that would take a job catching chickens or butchering chickens in the freezing cold plant would never stay at this job. I learned that those Americans who would take the job would, eventually, not return to work the next day.

Many clients came in their work scrubs and work boots, smelling like the chicken plant. They were cold, sometimes, still shivering from the temperature of the rooms where they stand in a line, cutting the chickens into parts. They are pushed to work as fast as possible in order to get the quota for the day. Their hands have carpal tunnel syndrome from the strain on their fingers wrapped around the scissors and the cutting shears. They are tired from standing all day long, but most of all, they are cold because the building must remain cold in order to process so many chickens.

The chicken catchers are another story. This is an awful dirty job, and one must be quick to move thousands of live chickens from the chicken houses into the large crates to be placed on the semitrucks that carry them to the processing plant. But I did not hear complaints from the people; they were so appreciative to have a job even though they were only paid minimum wage. Issues of legal status and lack of English was always the employer's "justification" to deny raises and offer upward career mobility and, so often, people stay in their position for years. Those who had become injured or had problems with circulation in the hands and feet were tended to by a doctor that was working right on site.

Those who had found their way to the eastern shore of Maryland and Delaware, were so grateful for their job even though they were paid minimum wage. They would rarely complain, except for those who wanted to move up the career ladder and obtain a raise—this was much more difficult to do. Issues of legal status and lack of English was always the reason to deny raises and, so often, people stayed in their position for years.

There was a big crackdown on undocumented immigrants working at some of these chicken plants during the Obama era, and many of the immigrants had to leave their jobs. Many of the workers did have documents, but they had been easily ordered from someone in North Carolina or sent for through the mail. They did not know whose name they had or social security number; all they knew was that, for a hundred and forty dollars, they now could work just by taking on a new identity. Some that I talked to did not even know they were doing something illegal. They just knew it was what you did to get your first job in the United States.

What happened during this crackdown, and after ICE had moved in, was that, suddenly, the poultry plants could not find enough workers to take their place. They had to cut their production until they were able to build up their workforce once more. I believe, during this time, many of the immigrants began to hire lawyers to help them apply for a work permit and asylum from their countries—the legitimate way. And by the way, it is almost impossible to obtain legal documents from these countries the *legal* way because of the high denial rate. On top of that, if the immigrant hires a lawyer and makes an application to the Department of Homeland Security, then of course, the government now knows who they are and has all their personal information, which makes deportation a possibility. The immigrant must then decide whether they want to take a chance in submitting their information in hopes of being granted asylum or a visa.

Each country is allotted so many visas each year and then they are gone. There are also not enough immigration lawyers and judges to handle all the applicants. The following is an article that addresses the backlog of citizenship cases in our country that I thought was interesting.

Regarding citizenship: "The backlog of citizenship applications is at the unprecedented amount of 753,352 applications as of the end of March 2018. At the current rate of processing applications, it would take USCIS over 25 years to get the current rate down to the Obama administration's backlog level of 380,639 applications in 2015, not including new applications. The "Second Wall," as NPA and its partners are calling it, is preventing hundreds of thousands of immigrants from becoming citizens and becoming voters. At the end of March 2018:

- New York City had a backlog of 81,206 applications

- Houston had a backlog of 42,341 applications
- Dallas had a backlog of 38,094 applications;
- San Francisco had a backlog of 27,481 applications
- Baltimore had a backlog of 20,485 applications
- Philadelphia had a backlog of 17,336 applications
- The District of Columbia had a backlog of 16,564 applications[3]

(Susana Flores, Sept. 17, 2018)

And the list goes on and on. Now isn't that interesting? Can our government not process these applications, which prevents more Latino representation and ability to vote? Interesting.

I began providing nonviolence classes to men batterers in Spanish and in English. In working with the men, I believe they were quite astonished that a white American woman was even teaching them anything. The cultural differences brought many discussions about why we Americans do what we do, what laws back up that treatment, and how to treat a woman with respect. The Latino men batterers taught me a lot also, for instance, slang words and explanations of cultural differences that explained what machismo was and the ability to even admit to their violence, which of course, was a must in these classes.

This job happened to be a good fit for me. First, it fell into my work as a *peace advocate* through my denomination and upheld my beliefs about nonviolence. I was able to *teach peace and respect* to a captive audience. I would not allow any of the students to minimize

---

[3] Flores, Susana. "Immigrant Rights Groups Sue US Citizenship and Immigration Services Over the Backlog of Citizenship Applications," Washington, DC, Susana@comunicationsshop.us, September 17, 2018.

their violence, collude, blame, or deny their violence of women. Any statement of such would be called out, and of course, it was hard for the men to accept at first, but little by little, they got the point and saw that these four things were not tolerated in class and in their daily lives. In the long run, they began to listen to themselves outside of the class and what they were saying and doing to their partners. They talked of taking responsibility for their actions and words. I had the men for twenty-six weeks or more, and so I do believe they left, at least, *thinking* a little differently—and I hoped that they would *act* differently around their loved ones or future loved ones. There is no guarantee that the men will actually change their behavior, but at least, I made sure they participated in the class and had food for thought.

For the Latino male, it was a little different because I was a woman, but on the other hand, I have been told that in the Latino population, they trust the outsider (American worker) more than their own. They told me that they were not aware of some of the laws in America and were appreciative and receptive to learning what the new laws were in the United States. Once trust was established, they would ask a lot of questions. Half of the problem was that not everyone receives a written handbook that tells a newcomer, "You may not beat your wife, you may not hit your children with a belt, and you may not drive without a driver's license, etc." Here, the law does have power—some may disagree on that, but coming from other countries where the law is useless, and the power is held by gangs and drug cartels, it is a lot different. Here in the United States, the police *do* something, and for that, most all immigrants are grateful! I heard many say they so appreciated the laws and rules of the land, once they knew what they were. Others told me that they were so grateful that immigration had found them at the USA border because they knew, at least, they were safe.

This class had a section on child discipline, male privilege, partnership, and respect among about twenty other things, and each person's behavior and reason for being in the class in the first place was called out, was processed, and looked at very closely. I hope that they left a better man after those classes, but I usually did not have the follow-up that was needed, so to tell you the truth, I really do not know the outcome.

In one of the classes, a man from Mexico told me that he had five children, and they were young. He told the class that his wife stayed home all day "resting" and not doing anything. He said he could easily do what his wife did—stay at home, watch the children, cook for them, and help them with their homework—oh, how easy that would be. A few weeks later, he came back to class with a strange look on his face. I asked him what the matter was, and he said, "My wife left me...with the children...and moved to California, and I am exhausted!" He said he could not believe how hard it was to get the kids bathed, dressed in the morning, and off to school, preparing meals, driving them to daycare, AND going to work. He said, "How is this even be possible? This is too difficult." And of course, he had a much better appreciation for his wife then but, by that time, had lost her.

I also provided therapy to women victims of domestic violence. I learned the disrespect and mistreatment of women is much different in each country, largely because of the lack of police protection in their countries. There is corruption, extortion, kidnapping, robbery, and bribery in their home countries, even by police. When one cannot even trust law enforcement and there is no police protection, the women are unable to protect themselves and are afraid to make police reports for fear of retaliation and to seek justice on the men who mistreat them. Many told me they had to escape secretly, with or without their children, so that they would not be killed. Many felt that there was nowhere else to run but to join their parents or other relatives who were already living in the United States. There was no time to apply for asylum in their country—so they ran north.

You might say that these stories are about gender violence, women's role versus men's roles, and how people are treated in the world. I learned that even though there are rapists and drug cartels at the border, most are innocent men, women, and children who are just concerned about one thing—their life and their safety. They are trying to avoid being killed AND are seeking a way to feed their families while some just want to be reunited with their family. Whatever happens is better than the death, hunger, and abuse that they had been suffering in their country. *The risk that they had to take to go over the border was not as great as the risk of staying where they were.*

The other thing that I hear often is that they are here because they prayed for help, and God brought them here! They give all the credit to God who has sustained them, given them strength and has given them courage to escape for their lives and make it to the United States. How can we, Americans, turn away someone who God has helped arrive here?

Not everyone is a rapist or a batterer as some politicians suggest, however, when you work with endless women who say they have been raped in their country, you see the overall picture of desperation and objectification of women. So many women tell me that they find their partner or husband who loves them for a while, but once she becomes pregnant, they leave her for another woman—leaving her at home to care for children, cook, and clean. This is a huge violation of respect and love. The life of these women is disregarded, and there is no protection from the authorities in town who have been "bought." So many men will have two or more partners outside the home, and the wife or the woman at home with the babies are the mothers to their children and the maid for the home.

Following are some of the stories that have been told over and over again to this worker, causing dismay and agony in writing as I record their tales, trying to help keep them in this country where they can be safe and secure, which is the goal for anyone facing such abuse. The only difference is that they are undocumented.

My belief is that love does not have borders, and the world does not have walls. We have created these things. Love does not create walls. God does not discriminate—and, in the end, will only look at the love and compassion in every person's heart. We are called to bring good into the world, not hatred, war, and disrespect. Everyone will have their judgment day. What is in our hearts is important. And to those who are seeking forgiveness, mercy, and justice, it is there waiting for us.

"Teacher," he asked, "which is the greatest commandment in the Law?" Jesus answered, "'You must love the Lord your God with all your heart, with all your soul, and with all your mind.' This is the greatest and the most important commandment. The second most important commandment is like it: 'You must love your neighbor as yourself.' The whole Law of Moses and the teachings of the prophets depend on these two commandments." (Matt. 22:36–40)

CHAPTER 8

If We Helped Cause It, We Should Help Fix It

I was talking with Officer Karen McNally, a police officer in Silver Spring, Maryland, who was passionate about her visits to Guatemala and her work with Guatemalans who had settled into the Eastern shore area. She cared very much about them and was helping them market their scarves made from rabbit hair. She had travelled to Guatemala several times and watched the women making the scarves personally. She gave me a scarf, and I treasured it. I never imagined that the people would capture my heart and soul also.

One Guatemalan, *Maria*, told me that she lived in a beautiful small *aldea*, on the rolling green hills of Guatemala. She was a beautiful young woman, with her long hair still wrapped into a braid down her back. She seemed timid, and her eyes told the story of mistrust, questioning everything that she heard and saw. She told me that she loved her town and did not want to leave it but felt that, as a teenager, she had no future there. There was extreme poverty and harsh living conditions. Women were still cooking on cement slabs with firewood that was scarce in her area. She could not afford to go to school although she had reached the sixth grade. She stopped going because she had to walk over two miles to get there every day, and it was very dangerous because of the men along the road who would attack the girls.

She explained that it was miles to find a doctor, and many people just use home remedies to treat their illnesses and wounds. The fields were filled with corn that her father grew, but only if there was enough rain. She and her siblings had to work from the age of eight to help harvest the *milpa* and other vegetables that they would sell in the market. Her family was large as she had eight brothers and sisters.

There was additional danger because the poppy fields were nearby. On the path to school were predators who are recruiting children to work in the poppy fields. This was so appealing to many because there were no other work opportunities for the children and young adults. Maria told me she wanted something better. She wanted to continue her education, and she wanted to help her parents and siblings so they would not have to struggle so much. She loved her country and did not want to leave, but she saw no other option. She was motivated and, through rumor, had heard about a place called the United States, the land of opportunity! So she came here!

I traveled to Guatemala in 1992, after traveling to El Salvador the week of the cease-fire. I was cautioned in going to Guatemala as it had been a dangerous place for even Americans. An American girl and her missionary team had been murdered as they were traveling through the country. But being young and adventurous, I was not afraid.

The Guatemalan exchange student who had come to our house as a boy was now a man, and an important one at that. He had wanted to become instrumental in fighting for the indigenous people just like his mother, who was also a politician. He had told me that, someday, he wanted to be president of Guatemala. His family had to flee Guatemala to England during the war because of their own threats of persecution. He had not become president but had travelled as ambassador of Guatemala in Russia and then the ambassador of Guatemala in South Korea. But at the time that I visited in 1992, he had a family and was living in Guatemala City.

When I visited them, their home was a little frightening to me as it had security walls built all around the house, and outside, "killer" dogs were barking (well, I'm not sure they were killer dogs, but they scared me). They were proud of their country and took me to the market to see all the beautiful artifacts and colorful souvenirs. I took pictures as any tourist would and did not really have the opportunity of going to the rural areas to see how the villagers lived.

But what I did was meet people who worked in the markets and were making the beautiful clothing as seen in pictures. I am fascinated by the indigenous people who are living a simple life and who have a heart of gold. The Guatemalan Indians were wearing the long dresses and white puffy sleeved blouses that have embroidery mixed in. The clothing, rugs, ponchos, and other artwork are just beautiful. One can tell that each thread is carefully sewn with care and precision. These threads have been passed down from generation to generation and brighten up the landscape, adding beautifully to the already luscious greenery and blueness of the countryside.

Now three decades later, I am working with the Guatemalan families who have fled this country. It used to be that the crime and corruption was mostly in the cities, but according to the people, there is no longer safety in the small mountainous towns. They feel that there is safety in the United States and that in this *great* country, they will find peace and be able to work. In Guatemala, there are little opportunities for a young person to work, especially if from the countryside.

Immigrants are coming into the United States every day. I do believe laws are created to be followed regarding immigration, and that open borders are not the answer. If only we could control the *root* problem, which are drugs, violence, extortion, need for power and control, lack of employment, and poverty. People would stay in their country that they love and thrive if they can work and care for their families. This is not an easy task, but until there are changes in the economy and security in the country, there will be people leaving to come north. I do not see a resolution to this happening any time soon. People are leaving everything they own and traveling for days seeking that peace and safety. They must be so desperate to risk their lives and give up everything they own, to walk across Mexico to seek this peace. The risk is not the pilgrimage to the United States but in living in a country where life can be robbed at any time.

There are no easy answers to any of those problems, and those who are running for political office say they are going to address those problems, but the corruption is so bad that they also have a hard time fighting the battle against evil. They are controlled by the bandits of the countries.

We cannot go back and change anything, but since the United States played such a huge role in the corruption and turmoil in the Central American countries in the '80s, funding the weapons for the war, supporting corrupt governments, and training the military, then we should help remedy the poverty and corruption there. It needs to be mentioned that the School of the Americas (now called the Western Hemisphere Institute for Security Cooperation) has been training the military from several Latin American countries, negative aspects that lead to torture and murder. This military training facility is located at Fort Benning, Georgia and continues today, training cadets from sixteen countries, to return to their countries to continue war and kill their own people. We have been protesting for years to have the training facility closed down. Why should the United States be involved in such atrocities, responsible for the death of many innocent people?

Guatemala's war, which ended in 1996, continues to deal with the thousands of people who returned from the war to find NO work. Those soldiers have most likely turned into being a corrupt police officer or a trafficker. Years later, the children of the wars are still struggling and trying to survive violence. It must be true, violence begets violence. Did the war accomplish anything but death and destruction? Are the people any better off today?

So the main problem for the average person in a third world country (if they still even use that term) is providing for the family and feeding the children. Hunger is caused by poverty and inequality, not scarcity. For the past two decades, the rate of global food production has increased faster than the rate of global population growth. The world already produces more than one and a half times enough food to feed everyone on the planet. But the people making less than two dollars a day—most of whom are resource-poor farmers cultivating small plots of land—can't afford to buy this food.[4]

The United States has enough food to feed the world. The United States has jobs to spare. Just look at all the people who do not want to work but want to sit on their front porch, use drugs, and take an easy ride. The Americans that I know personally will say to me, "But the illegals are taking all of our jobs away!" I don't know anyone who would offer to work in a field all day in the hot sun picking tomatoes or catching chickens to send to slaughter for minimum wage. I don't know of anyone who would like to work picking watermelons or grapes voluntarily. I do not personally know of anyone who has actually lost a job because of an immigrant. People are just scared and afraid of *losing their privilege and control*—all due to someone telling them they have been robbed of employment. I see "Help Wanted" signs every day that cannot be filled.

I work with the families every day, some who have been here for over ten or twenty years and who have raised their children here. They are working families, community based, who look out for each other, and support each other. Is it beneficial to deport an immigrant who has been working and paying taxes for ten to twenty years? Once immigrants are deported, they find themselves with less money than before and become easy recruits for street gangs or drug cartels, and America suffers the loss of *one less working body and taxpayer*. These people are *consumers* and *taxpayers* also; they are the ones who go out to eat, buy clothing, tools, and other supplies, and keep our small businesses alive.

---

[4] Holt-Gimenez, Eric, Contributor, Executive Director of Food First, "We already grow Enough Food for 10 Billion People– and Still Can't End Hunger," *Huff Post*/Life Study from McGill University and the University of Minnesota published in the journal *Nature*, 5/2/2012.

We should give each working family, who does not have a criminal record, a work permit and path to permanent residency in the United States. They should also be given the ability to travel back and forth to their country of origin because then, perhaps, many people would relocate voluntarily, especially the older generations who miss their native land and would like to spend the rest of their days there. Make visa applications a possibility, with decisions to be made quickly by the embassy. Reunite children who have been left behind to join their parents in the United States. Grant more funding to the CIA in controlling the drug traffic into the United States. Support law enforcement fighting criminals and traffickers at the borders and airways and highways and waterways.

The immigrant family who wants to work to support their families need to be commended for their contribution to society and granted that ability to flourish. Listen to their stories and have some compassion. The following stories are of real people with real fears. These are stories of immigrants who have come over the border seeking safe haven. The names and, sometimes, the places have been changed in order to avoid putting anyone into further danger as some individuals continue to be threatened in the United States.

The true measure of any society can be
found in how it treats its most vulnerable
members. (Mahatma Gandhi)

CHAPTER 9

Children Left Behind

The fact that more and more children are immigrating to the
United States is a result of *chain migration*, in that the children
are seeking out their parents who have already immigrated to the
United States. Families of the same town are following their friends,
neighbors, and relatives who have already left the country. Youth are
leaving their country because they do not see a future for themselves
in their country. Someone told me once that there was a huge bill-
board in El Salvador that advertised jobs in North Carolina! "Come
to North Carolina where there is work!" And the North Carolina
chicken plants were the ones who put it there!

The land is full of narco-traffickers, trying to recruit children at
a time when the country is already vulnerable to poverty and crime.
Some *children* are often trying to escape coercion into working with
the drug trade. Other young people decide that they need to escape,
seeking a brighter future. These are the children that we see entering
our country.

Many young individuals are also running from abusive aunts
and uncles and grandparents that have been caring for them after
their parents immigrated to the United States many years before.
Parents come to the United States, find a job, and then send money
back to their children so that they may attend school, since it costs
money to get their school supplies and shoes and uniforms. If there
is not enough money for these simple things, they are not permitted
to attend the school. Many children are desperate to find their par-

ents in the United States, and when there was an influx of children during the Obama years, this was actually a good thing because families were reunited, and children could finally meet their parents who gladly took responsibility for their own children. I have met many of those families, and the feeling is that of relief and extreme gladness of reuniting the family! The acculturation is often difficult, and adjustment takes a long time, but finally, parents and children are together again! If you think about it, a strong family creates a more stable and stronger country.

The dangers for children who are left behind are greater for the children whose parents are living in the United States. Gangs are prevalent and try to kidnap children who they may see are without a loving parent to protect them. They then try to force them to join their groups, knowing that children are more vulnerable when their parents are not around. Children whose parents are living in the United States are also targeted for ransom since gangs and traffickers believe that the children's parents who are living in the United States have money and will pay to keep their child alive.

Rita was living in the slums of Guatemala City, trying to earn enough money to support her daughter. She lived in a one-room apartment that had no security and broken facilities. She decided to leave her daughter behind in their small town because of her fear of being kidnapped in the city after receiving several threats. Rita said she finally decided to go to the United States because the crime was so great. She was aware of the dangers along the way and of the border area, but she decided to take the risk. She worked for one year cleaning houses in the city, saving money so that she could begin her journey, but she only made 1,000 *quetzals* a month. She said she would hear gunshots in the street all the time, and she knew there were gangs and drug traffickers everywhere.

Rita reported that while she was living in the capital in 2010, a gang kidnapped one of her thirteen-year-old nieces for three days. Their plan was to kidnap her and prostitute her in another country. Her niece was very traumatized by this, and when they brought her back, she could not talk about it without crying. Her niece was only able to escape when the men were drunk one night and fell asleep, and she made her way to San Marcos where she went to the police station. She stated that the police would not investigate or do anything and told her she would have to bribe them. Just knowing this has caused much fear for the family.

Rita reported that in 2012, they threatened her also. They said they wanted a portion of the money that she made at the end of every month, and if she did not pay them, she would be killed. She said they called this a "quota." In 2013, she decided it was time to leave and join her family who was already in the United States. She traveled by foot for one month to reach the United States border. Her daughter continued to live with her mother in Guatemala, but the gangs continued to bother her mother and daughter.

In March of 2016, Rita said that her daughter, who was then seven years old, had gone with her grandmother to the market and was almost killed by the gangs in the city. They had threatened to kidnap and rape her seven-year-old daughter if Rita did not pay $5,000. Rita showed me a picture of the newspaper article which showed a picture of her daughter who had been attacked by a man who told her, "I am going to take you and rape you and kill you." Rita said her daughter ran, but she was hit in the head with a machete. Her mother, who was there also, screamed and started yelling, and the man also hit her mother in the head. When her mother started running, he hit her again two more times. The neighbors came to help them, finding both on the ground unconscious. The neighbors sent them to a hospital that was two hours away because the injuries were so severe. According to Rita, the delinquents were caught and put in a detention center for one week, but the authorities let them go because they were young and underage.

Rita's mother was afraid to go back to their home, but they returned to the house eventually. Her daughter does not want to return to school because she had been so traumatized. She does not want to go out of the house and does not want to play with other children. She trembles and cries when she sees people that she does not know. She tells her Rita that she is afraid for her safety, and she begs to come to join her in the United States. She misses her mother and is scared.

Rita stated that this has been very hard for her and her mother. Rita wants her daughter to receive psychological help because the trauma has changed her and her grandmother's life completely. On top of that, she stated that her daughter's head continues to hurt where they hit her. When her daughter sleeps at night, she is yelling, jumping in her sleep, and cannot sleep because of the nightmares. Rita cries that this hurts because she cannot do anything except try to bring her here to live with her in the United States. Rita wants to bring her daughter here so badly, and this is why she is applying for asylum for her and her daughter.

Drug cartels and poverty, abuse and extortion are all bad. But one of the saddest things for me is to see and hear stories of children who have been neglected or who have never had a mother or father say "I love you" to them. The neglect is caused by the parents who may leave their children with a family member or friends, with the plan of bringing their children to join them later. Parents are so desperate to seek a new life for their children. Many children tell me that money sent to the relatives who are caring for them are used to purchase food, but the food will only be given to their own children. The children left behind, who have suffered neglect and lack of affection, grow up to be adults who are seriously damaged emotionally and unable to recover easily. There are abandonment issues of not being able to fully love because of their lack of trust or the feeling of being unloved as a child.

Marcos was born in Ixchiguan, Guatemala, which is the part of the country that Tajumulco is fighting. He told me that when he lived in Guatemala as a young boy, he was brought up by both sets of grandparents because both of his parents had immigrated to the United States when he was only two years old. He said that the hardest part growing up was wondering why he *had no parents*. He never knew his father, but he had met his mother later, only to have her leave again, and he continued to live with his grandparents.

He said he would go to school and see other children with their mother and father, and this would make him so sad, and sometimes, he admits he even felt anger for being left behind. Although he lived with his grandparents, he did not feel that he could talk to them, and he craved the love of a mother or father to be by his side.

Marcos said that their family lived way out in the country, and he would have to walk almost two hours to get to school. This was difficult for a young child, and as he got older, the gang members began to grab him and talk to him about working for them. He said that they wanted him to work with them harvesting the *amapola* (poppy plants) and would threaten to hurt him or his family if he did not go with them. The first decision he had to make was to not go to school anymore. But the gang still knew all about him, where he lived, and who his grandparents were. He said he was afraid to tell his grandparents because he was afraid the men would do something to him. He said he had to deal with this almost on a daily basis when he went to school.

One time, while he was still in school, they grabbed him and said they were going to cut off his fingers. They even tried to cut his hand off, but a man was walking by and tried to help him, and they then ran away. The men who had threatened him had their heads covered, so he did not know where they were. He said that, many times the crooks would cut off fingers of the people as a form of torture.

He told me that he had a cousin who had been killed by the same bandits. They took him when he was nineteen years old and killed him because he did not want to work with them. The story is that they went to look for him, found him, tied him up to a pole, beat him, stoned him, poured gasoline on him, and burned him alive. They did this to him and his friend. The drug dealers/traffickers threatened the townspeople, "If you don't do what we want, this will happen to you." Their mothers both stood by in agony and despair as their sons were killed. Marcos said it was so terrible, and no one could do anything about it. The gang members would tell the townspeople, "If you try to take them to the hospital, we will do the same to you." Where were the police? The police, in this case, had no power to do anything either, and Marcos said that they probably had been bribed or paid off.

At the age of twelve, Marcos then decided that he could not continue go to school anymore and decided to live alone. He ran away from his grandparents' home, thinking that they would be safer if he were not there, and found an empty hut where he and two other children lived. They took care of each other; none had parents in the country.

Marcos said that he did not come to the United States because of the work but because of the fear and the crime, the violence, and the anger that he had against his own parents who had abandoned him. He told me he had to depend upon himself and God for strength. He said he did not have any money but decided to take the risk because he wanted a happy family someday, something he was deprived of. He thanks this country for opening their doors to him. He wanted to have a better life.

He came here when he was seventeen years old, and today, he is twenty-five years old and has one child. Marcos states that, even though the cartels encouraged him to work for them, his biggest challenge was growing up without the love of his parents. He said the bad people were always playing with his emotions, and he had nowhere to escape. He said he has seen a lot of things but has not had a *true family* until now. In the United States, he feels safe and secure. He feels that he can completely support his family and raise his child in a good environment. When he was growing up, he would see families together and wonder why he could not have a family. He would ask God why. He feels that there must be a reason, and perhaps, he can help other people who were in the same situation someday. He knows that he wants to help others and to be a part of a larger mission.

Marcos said that he feels that his life would be in danger if he returns because it is a place where they know everyone and would remember him. He says his biggest fear is to lose his family and that his child would have to live the kind of life that he had grown up with. He feels, if he returns to his county, he would always be hiding and fending for his life.

Sara was also a victim of neglect, but in a different way. She felt completely rejected by her mother, and at age seven, her mother began acting differently. They lived in a little one-room house, and it was overcrowded, and there were so many children that there was not a moment when she could receive special attention from her mother. Sara said that, perhaps at age seven, she became more aware of her emotions at this age. She became depressed and alone when she could not spend any special time with her mother; there were no special "family" outings, only yelling in the home.

At the age of seven, her mother told her that her "father" was not her biological father and that he had wanted to poison her. She said her stepfather wanted her mother to kill her, so her mother took her down to the river to drown her (but did not follow through). Sara told me that she could not get this out of her mind. She remembers the hut that they lived in and the path through the hillside that led to the water. She remembers the trauma of feeling that she was going to die and that she was in great danger. All she wanted all her life was for someone to love her and care for her. Then her mother and stepfather left her with a relative who abused her and her siblings, often not giving them any food. She felt completely abandoned and could not talk to anyone.

Sara was raped at the age of nine by an eighteen-year-old cousin. This happened on several occasions, and she did not know what to do and felt she had no one to talk to. She continues to have disturbing memories and nightmares. After that, she did not want to live.

At the age of seventeen, Sara tried to commit suicide by cutting her wrist, but a friend found her. She told me that she had not resolved the rape and the lack of love that she felt by her mother. All of this caused her to want to end her life. When Sara wanted to get married, her parents told her, "Go ahead, you can do whatever you want. We do not care." Sara reported sadness that she could not even share her happiness with them.

Over time, Sara reported that she gave birth to five children. She knows that she was seeking the love that she never knew through her children, but then had to support them somehow, so she immigrated to the United States. She talks to her children as often as she can and tells them how much she loves them. Secretly, she told me that she did not think she could be a good parent to them because she did not know how and has never spent much time with them as she went back to work soon after each child was born. She realized that she did not know how to parent because of her own poor role models but sends money to their caregivers who support her children so that they are able to go to school. Sara said she did not know how to nurture or interact with her children then because she did not know how to be a loving parent.

Little by little, the children are making it to the United States, seeking their parents. The reason for the immigration has nothing to do with sponging off United States social services or gaining an economic advantage as some would have the American public believe, but they are coming because of the spiked violence in their countries, seeking safety in any and all surrounding nations throughout the region. Parents wanting to protect their children from death are sending them to seek political asylum, even in neighboring nations such as Mexico, Nicaragua, Panama, and Costa Rica.

Children are encountering many barriers and, if not arriving at the border with an actual parent, are being detained while their caregiver is vetted. Realize that if the children's parents are already living in the United States, they will be arriving with other people and other caregivers. What they need is to be joined with their parents. These children, once they have reached their parents, need counseling as they strive to resolve the trauma that they have encountered over the years. This counseling requires someone who can speak their language, establish a trusting relationship, and who is trained in trauma therapy. Teenagers as well as younger children are struggling with their past but also with the new culture, the peers at their schools, and the racism that they face by other American students and community. It is my hope that they find their family and be treated with respect for all they have lived through and be treated with kindness.

Definition of downtrodden:
Oppressed, persecuted, subdued,
repressed, crushed, enslaved,
burdened, exploited, disadvantaged,
underprivileged,
victimized, abused, misused, ill-
treated, powerless, helpless

CHAPTER 10

Seeking Peace

Women are constantly left with the responsibility of providing for their children. By helping the women, we are helping a complete unit. Women are used, abused, and taken advantage of, but they continue to fight for their rights. When left alone with children and with no financial support, it is even more difficult. Many of the women I met had been "married," taken to the husband's mother's house, impregnated, left there locked in the house, and then the "husband" would leave to find their lovers. This does not happen with all men and women, but MOST of the women told me the same story. The women feel that their purpose is to be used for sex, bear children, cook the meals, and clean the house, while the husbands drink away their earnings and find another partner to enjoy.

Roberta realized she could not survive in Honduras alone with six children. The children did not have shoes, clothing, or food. She would work washing clothes and folding clothes to earn a little bit of money, but it was not enough to support the children or send them to school. This was when she decided to talk to her own father about watching the children so that she could go to the United States. She felt that she had to leave.

Roberta said she planned on going to the United States for a short time and then return to her children, but it did not happen that way, because over the years, her children eventually immigrated to the United States to be with her, one by one. At the time of this writing, Roberta has been in the United States fifteen years. She admits that she has also suffered a hard life here in the United States, but she is appreciative of the ability to work, be productive, and live in peace. Now *all* her children are here with their spouses whom they have met here, and she has many grandchildren that she would never want to leave.

Roberta told me that she could not find work in the United States in the beginning, and her daughter did not want to go to school because she worried so much about her mother. Although her daughter's father was not in the United States, she continued to suffer and struggled to make ends meet but was happy to be able to raise her children without the help of an abusive man. At least, they have a home to live in, food, and clothing. For this reason, she has applied to remain in the United States legally.

Nancy cried as she told me her story of escaping gangs. She is a pretty young girl with long black hair, who told me that she had become pregnant at the age of fifteen. She said that both she and her boyfriend were living together and studying, but they realized that things were not working out for them, and the *Maras* (gang) kept bothering her. Nancy said that when she was pregnant, she moved next door to Tapachula, Mexico, to seek medical help because there were are no resources where she lived in Guatemala. She heard that there was work there, and during this time, she gave birth to a baby girl while working in her employer's house.

Even while pregnant, men from the gang would grab at her and assault her. She told them that she was pregnant, hoping that they would go away; they never raped her, but she said they would not stop bothering her and wanted her to go with them.

She told me that, one time, there was a boy riding in the bus, and he was laughing with two other men from Malacatán. The *mareros* took him out of the bus and cut his neck. She said that the boy was innocent and only going to visit his grandmother. She said that everyone in town was terrified. The man who cut his neck was found but only held for three months because *someone paid off the police to let him go.* Nancy reported, "We wanted justice but could not get it. *The authorities could not do anything.*" Therefore, she is seeking asylum; she could not escape the threats of rape and abduction in her country and felt that the only thing she could do would be to seek asylum in the United States.

Since 2009, Homeland Security, and the border patrol have teamed up with local law enforcement agencies throughout the United States and began an accelerated campaign of deporting undocumented immigrant parents. I saw families who lost the bread-winner in the family by deportation. I have heard of deportees who were killed as soon as they arrived in their country because they were victims of extortion and could not produce enough money quick enough. Families were being ripped apart, creating orphans of their children as legal United States-born citizens. Obama removed illegal immigrants at nine times the rate of just twenty years ago, far more than any other president. Two million of the undocumented have, in fact, been removed already. Regardless of how long a person may be residing in America and regardless of having a family here, being a law-abiding productive citizen, it makes no difference. Upon return-ing, the deported are frequently persecuted, tortured, and murdered. The hardship and tragedy bought down on so many hardworking taxpaying families are anything but humane and compassionate. It pains me to see Americans who have such cold hearts.

Tajumulco and Ixchiguan are two areas in Guatemala that have been fighting over land for decades. The war in Central America, funded by the United States, took the lives of thousands of inno-cent people. It was the United States who provided ammunition and training to the soldiers for "killing fields" of indigenous peo-ple. Before that, the Spaniards had conquered the Aztec Indians. The people in this country continue to be abused, tortured, discriminated against, and taken advantage of, now by their own people and by neighboring countries.

Angela told me that her family was very poor and did not have money, but when her father started getting ahead economically from his farming, the gangs started threatening them because they knew/ thought they had money. Criminals and gangs threatened to kill her parents and take what they had, and Rita became very afraid.

Angela said that the people in this area were fighting over land, and when she was little, she would hear shootings from far away, but then they would find bullet holes in their house. Angela explained that, one day, someone tried to rob the home during the day, but the children that were there started screaming, and all the neighbors came to help them which prevented the robbery. But the robberies and kidnappings continued.

Soon, the children were not allowed to play outside, and people could not cross into certain territories and would prohibit passage over their land. She said that many houses were burned down. There were curfews on the town, and most people do not go out after six at night because of the risk of being killed.

Angela said that, one day, the bandits went into a little seven-year-old girl's house that lived just fifteen miles from their house and killed her. She said they were also shooting at her family, and so they could not leave the house for three days, which meant they could not bury the little girl as is custom to do within forty-eight hours. She said that this happened in 2010, but there has been constant fighting over the land, and their family was threatened often. They were warned that they would torture them and rape the women if they crossed into their territory. Angela said that they lived with this fear all the time and could never live or feel at peace. She said the bad people would be in the mountains with masks on, hiding and ready to shoot anyone who went through there, even school children walking to school. The fighting over this land *continues today.*

All these individuals and families are seeking peace in their lives. They are fleeing the threat of violence, crime, and poverty in their countries, but the biggest reason is the inability to see a positive future for their children in their countries. What is the solution? We only have two choices. We can refuse to help those seeking asylum, essentially causing more poverty, destruction, and death for those who are fleeing for their lives, or we take the humanitarian route and attack the base problem of why individuals are leaving in the first place, turning around corrupt governments and the flow of money (since everything usually comes down to money and greed), and we help create safety in the communities—a place where people want to live in peace—while continuing to grant asylum of the cases that deserve to receive asylum. Since we, the United States, created and supported the problem in the '80s by funding the war on both sides, then perhaps, we need to find ways to correct the reasons for the mass exodus from the Central American/Mexican triangle and help turn around the poverty and crime that our brothers and sisters are facing today. I choose the second option.

Carefully watch your thoughts, for they
become your words. Manage and watch your
words, for they will become your actions.
Consider and judge your actions, for they
have become your habits. Acknowledge and
watch your habits, for they shall become your
values. Understand and embrace your values,
for they become your destiny. (Ghandi)

CHAPTER 11

Domestic Violence

Almost every story that I hear includes some form of domestic violence in one way or another. This is a problem that all societies have and is yet to be conquered. Domestic violence in European countries in the 1800s and earlier included the ideology of women and children being a man's property. The abuse and murder of women and children was commonplace and accepted. The husband and father could inflict punishment on any member of his household for any reason. Whenever women and children are seen as "belonging" to a man, violence has been used as a tool of control. In many of the South and Central American countries, women in society are used and abused and taught that their bodies are for any man who wants to take them. This is clearly the case, not only in the South and Central American culture, but other countries worldwide.

I find it interesting that The American Society for the Prevention of Cruelty to Animals (ASPCA) was founded before child abuse laws were founded. The ASPCA was founded in 1866, and several months later, the first meeting of the Society for the Prevention of Cruelty to children was held at the ASPCA's office.[5] The American Humane Association also works to end animal abuse and child abuse. Thus began the laws against abuse and domestic violence in the United States.

In 1994, Joe Biden created the Violence Against Women Act, which decreased domestic violence by 64 percent from 1994 to 2010 (Biden, September 10, 2014), protecting women and children alike.[6] But many countries have not caught up to us yet, and women will tell you that they have nowhere to turn. I am told that the town officials, police, and politicians are corrupt and unable to control the perpetrators of violence.

Rosa was born in a rural area of Guatemala and is forty-three years old. Rosa understands that she had another seven-year-old sister that had died of neglect and lack of attention but does not understand more than that.

Rosa said that, at age fifteen, she fell in love with the father of her children and began to live with him at age sixteen. She reported that she had her first child, and they were happy, but after she had her second child, problems started.

When she had her third child, her husband began to threaten her, saying that if she did not have a son, he would leave her. He began to beat her often and was always threatening her. After she had a baby boy, her husband continued to beat her. She said that he would leave frequently, come home drunk, and then hit her. Soon, the children noticed the violence, and they would be beaten also. She could not understand why. She did not know about birth control and why the men in her life had turned on her, treating her as an object.

This is a common story with so many of the women I have interviewed. Rosa said her husband would punch her in the face, pull her long hair, drag her by her hair, push, kick, and would use a belt to hit her legs. She said he continually threatened her life, and she felt so afraid to be near him. He would humiliate her and call her

---

[5] Loar, "Why Human Service Professionals Should Pay Attention to Cases Involving Cruelty to Animals," in Child Abuse, Domestic Violence, and Animal Abuse, supra, note 1 at 121.

[6] Biden, Joe, "Domestic Abuse," *Time* Magazine, Sept. 10, 2014.

names and make her feel guilty. Rosa innocently questioned why her husband had changed during their time together. She also decided to escape his wrath to join her sisters in the United States who had also fled abusive husbands.

Juanita was referred to my office by a community service organization working with victims of domestic violence and the local police department after a near-death experience when her boyfriend tried to kill her by *strangulation*. Juanita told me of the night that her boyfriend wrapped his hands around her neck and squeezed until *he* became afraid that he may have killed her. This happened to her in the United States.

Juanita was very timid and anxious and had a flat affect as she spoke about her near-death experience. She said that she thinks she actually died and was not conscious again until her boyfriend tried to give her CPR and poured water on her face. He took her to the hospital, where she was sent home without knowing the real story.

The following Thursday, she went to the doctor because she was not feeling well, and her primary care physician noticed that her eyes were filled with blood due to hypoxia and asked her to tell the truth about what had happened. He reported the incident to the police, and her boyfriend was arrested and deported for attempted first-degree murder.

When I looked at Juanita, she appeared traumatized and was staring straight ahead with bloodshot eyes. She told me that she felt very little emotion and was having nightmares. She said she had a loss of memory and could not make decisions. She felt that she had completely changed as a person. She reported that her emotions were numb but felt grateful that she was alive. Juanita continues to show slow movements.

After this incident, Juanita began to receive threats by the perpetrator's mother. This often happens to victims of abuse who turn in their perpetrator. The abuser's family will also turn on the victim, making the victim feel even more isolated. They often threaten saying, "If you ever return to your country, we will hurt you/kill you."

Juanita continuously reports that she feels great sadness at work; her eyes sting and are red at work, and this reminds her of the near-death experience. She said she wants to cry but her *tears are stuck in her throat*. Juanita reports an intense fear and hatred for men at this time. She does not like talking to others and gets mad when people try to joke around with her. She feels she has become more courageous in her personal relationships, in some respects, but more serious.

Adriana was nineteen years old when I first met her. She looked humble and had her head down as she talked in a low voice. She told me that her life as a child consisted of a lifetime of violence. Her parents always fought, and the children were frequently beaten. According to Adriana, they never shared as a family, and all the brothers and sisters were all afraid of their parents. Her oldest sister was the first to immigrate to the United States, followed by her three younger brothers and then herself, and it was all because of the abuse that they endured in their hometown as children.

Adriana reported that her father's treatment to her, her siblings, and her mother was severe. Her father would beat the children with a belt and even threaten the children with the machete. Her father insulted the children and mother by telling them that they were not worth anything.

She cried as she told me that, one day, her father threatened her and her mother with a machete. He told her mother to leave the house with the children, or he was going to take them out dead. Adriana reported that her family lives in a very small town, and that everyone is fighting over the land and the water in the area. She also stated that other families are always trying to get them to leave the area, and she had never received any support from them. Her family had never lived in peace. She said they had heard that there was a place called the United States, where people were free, and one could live in peace. *She did not know anything about immigration laws or permission to enter the United States.* She said that she and her siblings all came to the United States out of love for their mother and to be able to give their mother a better life.

Beatriz was sixteen years old when I talked to her. She said that there were many problems in their home as her father would continuously mistreat her mother. Beatriz's mother did all that she could to protect her youngest two children from their father, and she told me that her father did not hit her as much as the older siblings because her mother tried to protect the smallest children. Beatriz's other siblings, who were more brutally abused, moved out of the house to escape their father's wrath at the age of twelve years old.

Beatriz reported that, sometimes, the police would be called, but they would not do anything to protect the women or children from abuse. At the same time, their father would call the police to take the family out of his house, but to her advantage, the police did not act on this either. One day, her mother went to the court to put an order of arrest on him. So the police came and then arrested him for nonpayment of child support. Shortly after, they allowed him to leave the jail because he said he would pay, but he never did. Since he did not pay, they told him to leave the family in the house. Finally, Beatriz reported that she could not stand it any longer. She left Guatemala, without telling her mother or father, to seek refuge and arrived in the United States, entering as a minor.

Beatriz reported that she has been in the United States for a short time, but she finally feels that she is safe. She has her aunt and her uncle and a church congregation who is helping her to become resettled. She is attending a high school and likes school. Most of her siblings are in Mexico, and others are still suffering with her mother in Guatemala.

The role of women in Guatemala, as stated earlier, brings "justified" abuse to the women. Linda had to put up with similar roles of women as seen by men. She reported that her life was good when she was very young, but when she turned eleven, her father told her that *she was not preferred or important as much as a male.*

Linda was eleven years old when she experienced bullying in school. The kids called her fat and other names. She said she did not want to go because many of the kids picked on her and wanted to hit her. Even though she had gotten good grades, *her father said that girls only get out of school to find a husband and have babies.* So she stayed out of school the next year.

Linda's brother, who was in the United States, encouraged her to go back to school and told her that he would support her financially. He knew that she was doing well in math, science, art, and all the subjects. She went to school just on the weekends because it was cheaper that way. She studied a total of nine years.

Then the *worst* happened. When she started to study, her father introduced her to a man that worked on the farm. She said that everything was beautiful to her. One day, this man started to talk to her and told her he had a beautiful field to show her. The man said it would not take long to see it, so she said okay. She reported that she decided to go with him to a location five minutes from her house. He took her to a building that did have pretty curtains and a window looking out to a very pretty field of *milpa*. She cried, "I was only thirteen years old when he hurt me." As Linda was talking to me, she began to *dissociate as she talked of the rape.* She explained tearfully that she tried to leave, but he would not let her. He threatened that if she told her dad, her dad would hit her, and all the kids would hit her. Linda admitted that she was scared because her older sister had gotten married and then pregnant when she was sixteen, and her mother had hit her for that. She did not want to be hit. She felt that she could not tell her mother or her father. This man continued to abuse her every weekend when she went to school. With time, she stated that she became numb and would just shut her eyes and dissociate.

This went on for one and a half years. Soon after that, she reported that the man got tired of her and did not look for her as much. By that time, much damage had been done. Linda decided to come to the United States because her father's worker had returned, and her father would say to him, "Maybe someday you will be in love with my daughter." Her father did not know how this man had hurt her so much, both physically and emotionally.

She later had a boyfriend who wanted to marry her. She thought he was a farmer, but later, she found out that he was a drug trafficker. He also knew that she had a pass to cross over the border of Guatemala into Mexico. At one point, he wanted her to pass drugs. His enemies were all friends of hers. She did not want any problems.

Linda decided that she wanted to leave Guatemala because of all her problems, but she had no money. Her dad's worker wanted her to be his mistress, and another man wanted to marry her. She told her brother that if she went, she would give one part of her land to him, so this was how she paid for the trip. Her boyfriend wanted to marry her that Saturday, so she left that Tuesday without telling anyone. She left alone at the age of fifteen.

These stories may be the same as stories of young women in the United States. The difference is that the United States has laws and a system to deal with crime. In Guatemala, there is nowhere to turn. How do we stop injustice in another country? Do we have the right to interfere? If we allow injustice to continue, we are responsible for the continued problems. If everyone stood up to denounce violence, perhaps there would be hope for a more peaceful world. How do we, as a "responsible" country as strong as the United States, influence the well-being in a country such as Guatemala, El Salvador, Honduras, Mexico, or any other country when it is not our country? How can we diminish poverty, hunger, and violence throughout the world when there continues to be the lust for riches, gold, and power? That is the question.

A different world cannot be built
by indifferent people.

CHAPTER 12

Human Trafficking

Cases of human trafficking happen where women are vulnerable and feel that they have no choice. Some women have been kidnapped, sold, and used for sexual favors, while others have had to choose whether to be used so they can feed their children. Women become victims of domestic violence, partner abuse, and forced prostitution, often enduring emotional and physical strain. When a woman is knocked down so often and left with no self-esteem, they are more easily exploited and used, jailed and often separated from children for a period of time as seen by the case below.

I do not believe that anyone denies there are bad people at the border and elsewhere in any country. I do not believe that anyone advocates for the "bad" person to enter the United States, contrary to what our president says. Perhaps our attention should be more on those causing violence instead of denying asylum to the victims of trafficking, abuse, and crime.

Women and children are falling victim to human trafficking, prostitution, and child slavery throughout the world. This has become a global problem, but it is also happening in our own backyards. I have had a fifteen-year-old child tell me that she would go down to the corner store right here in small town USA, and then sent to a man's house almost every weekend. Her mother thought she was working at the store after making friends with the store owner there. This was quickly addressed, but there are women who are brought into the country with the agreement that she stay with the man who brought her, work at a farm job or chicken farm, and turn over all earnings to the man. Often, these cases are the hardest cases to work with because the women fear deportation or reprisals if they cooperate with the police. Shelters are being set up now to help hide and shelter the women from further intimidation by their abusers.

Carolina met her first partner from Guatemala, who was living in Chiapas but was already married and had chosen her as his lover. He abused her, demoralized her, and treated her harshly. When she became pregnant, he became very angry and tried to hide her from the public and tried to force her to abort the baby. After the first month of pregnancy, she left this man and had her first child.

Her second partner was the father of her second child and was also a very violent person and abusive. The only reason that she stayed with him was because of his constant threats to her until, one day, he threw hot soup on her shoulders and head, severely burning her. The abuse included threats to kill her and refusal to allow her to leave her home, telling her that if she did not do what he said, he would kill her daughter also (which was also his daughter). She remained with him four years while the abuse worsened until she finally was able to escape. These relationships caused her to be very fearful of men and were only a prelude to what happened to her physically and emotionally in the following years.

Carolina carries memories and physical scars to prove her victimization by men, and she said she was also a child victim of sexual abuse. She told me, at age sixteen, a neighbor coerced her into having sex by blackmailing her. She told me that she would walk down the path to her house, and the older man lured her to his house by telling her that he needed help in reading a letter. This was her first experience at feeling vulnerable and violated sexually.

After she was finally able to leave her abusive partner, she fell into the hands of a Mexican pimp known as El Lobo (also known as El Diablo) while being held hostage by him in a brothel in the south. Carolina had been at a dance and was approached by a man who took an interest in her and then followed her home without her knowing it. He told her he knew where she lived and where her children were, all the time threatening her to go with him or her children would be hurt. They had only spoken to each other two times, and the third time, he asked her to go work for him in this restaurant. Since she needed a job and felt weak at the time, desperately needing employment in order to feed her children, she went to the restaurant.

The man obligated her to get involved with prostitution and with him sexually, or he said he would kill her family. He put her in a house with other men who paid for sexual services for three days and would not allow her to leave, which meant that her children did not know where she was. The plan was that she was supposed to be there eight days and then he was to take her to another town for another eight days. She was not permitted to leave even though she begged to go home because her children were alone.

He told her she had to have sex with the men who came in, charging them $25 each—$12 was to go to the owner of the house, and $13 was to go to el Lobo. She would not receive anything. If there were any tips, she was to also collect this and put it in a separate envelope. She was not allowed to keep any money for herself. She was instructed to hide all evidence, throwing all condoms down the toilet, however, since she was new and did not understand the significance of this, she placed all the incriminating evidence into a trash can. She was so scared and afraid because he had told her that he knew where her children lived, and he threatened to hurt her family if she did not do what he said. She had heard that El Lobo had also killed his wife and a child in Chiapas in the past, so she was very afraid of him. Therefore, she did what she did. She had wanted to call the police, but he said he would know.

Somehow, the police were informed about the operation, and when they finally came, they put her in jail, not believing her or listening to her when she tried to explain that she was a "prisoner" in hands of the man. But there was no proof that she was being forcefully raped and had been imprisoned except for the evidence collected in her room.

Carolina reported feeling completely humiliated and ashamed at the events of her abuse and rape. Men have degraded her, telling her she is ugly and worthless. If she did not want to do what they wanted, they would humiliate her and hurt her. El Lobo's friend was the first one to come into her room the first day to "test" her out, asking for extreme sex as she pleaded with him. He treated her so badly that she just cried and cried. When she tried to refuse him, he said he would tell El Lobo, and she was terrified.

After the police raided the brothel and took Carolina into custody, they were unable to find El Lobo because of lack of information or clues. Carolina felt very much a victim of the system that she was in. She was already in anguish and pain, and when the police came, there was no sympathy for her health or the well-being of her children. She did not know if El Lobo was after her children or if she was in more danger. She suffered when thinking about this and cried because she had no one to turn to. She felt tortured emotionally and was dying of fear from El Lobo.

When the police came, they did not talk to her or ask her any questions. Her children would cry and ask her to come home. They didn't know where she was. She stated that she carried so much heartache at the hands of men; they have only been violent with her, abusive, and forceful. This all happened in 2008.

Carolina was presented with problems in almost every life area. She could not work because of her low educational level, limited English, and pending immigration status. She became forgetful easily during emotional strain. She showed many signs of post-traumatic stress disorder and depression. Carolina had a difficult time going to sleep and then, when sleeping, did not sleep well. She had nightmares about being in jail with the man (El Lobo) who was prostituting her and controlling her with threats. She dreamt that she and her children would be killed or thrown in water, or that someone is going to take her children away.

Luckily, this woman and her children were eligible for a T-Visa, which is a visa available to those victims of trafficking. Today, she has permanent residency. She is healthy and happy and employed. Her children are doing well in school, and she hopes that El Lobo has been captured. She completely cooperated with police, and this was what qualified her for the T-Visa. Because of her residency, she can work legally, and her children are happy and doing well in school.

Human trafficking is a form of modern-day slavery. "Once you lose your free will, you are a slave." It is a crime when a person uses force or coercion to control another person for the purpose of engaging in sexual acts or services against their will.

Among the most devastating consequences for victims is that they feel that they are not safe anymore, not a good person, and that the world is not just or meaningful. Many times, they lack support of family and friends because of the negative stigma attached.

It is important to recognize the signs and symptoms of the woman who may be a victim of trafficking. Often they are not permitted to speak for themselves or go into the public alone.

This happened in our clinic. A woman walked in, avoiding eye contact with a sense of fear about her, and then the man insisted on entering every medical examination with her.

Women who come into the office, seeking help for depression or anxiety, showing signs of physical injuries or abuse and who may appear to be malnourished, could be at risk for trafficking.

It is important as a social worker, health care provider, or even a friend to be aware of the signs of trafficking and to seek the appropriate resources to be able to protect these women from further harm. Most of all, it is important to believe them when they say they are being *used* for profit or being held captive. You could be saving a life.

Your wound is where your light
enters you! Nonconsensual.

CHAPTER 13

Breaking the Cycle of Abuse
The Story of Maria

Child abuse is not at all controlled in other countries as it is in the United States, and the stories are grim. If anyone ever wonders why the laws of the United States are so strict and criticize the social workers who are removing the children from their homes, it is because of stories like these. Children have suffered long enough, and finally, there are laws to protect them. In other countries, even if the abuse is to be reported, rarely are police or other officials able to control the crimes because of lack of power or bribery on the part of the perpetrators. So many adults that I counseled came for therapy only after suffering years of abuse or neglect, and none of it had been discussed with anyone. They were either too ashamed of what had happened or afraid of further abuse if anything was mentioned. For many, therapy was not even an option in their communities, and the stigma was so large that it would have been the last option for them.

One of the worst cases that I ever worked with was a woman named Maria that I have worked with for years. She would always call me Doctora, even though I had told her on numerous occasions that I was not a doctor. However, for her, out of respect and appreciation for the years of counseling, she continued to call me Doctora. This is a story of Maria and her husband. She gave me specific permission to allow her story to be told because she is now speaking out about her life and how, even in the worst conditions, one could turn a terrible life into a positive ending. Her story has turned into a positive message for all those women who have suffered from years of abuse as a child, and she wanted me to tell her story. When I asked her the big question *why*, she answered, "So that all women understand that there is help available, and that they do not have to suffer all of their lives."

Maria has been in the United States now for over fifteen years and is desperately struggling to obtain asylum because if she would return to her country of Mexico, she would most certainly run into the men who had abused her for years. She first came to me seeking counseling for sexual abuse, referred from a nearby community center.

Maria explained that she had been sexually abused since the age of eight by her alcoholic father, by her grandfather, later by her first husband, and then by the men that her husband had "sold" her to. She had witnessed her father controlling and beating her mother for years, and she imagines that is why her mother could not protect her from her father.

Maria said that her father was very possessive and would throw food out when drunk. When he was angry, he withdrew food from the children, causing the children to go hungry. Maria said that she felt like dying most of her young life because of the severe weekly sexual abuse by her father. Maria said that she *never slept* after he would attack her at night as she lay next to her mother. She would put covers around her head in order to avoid him. She reported that her mother did not, and possibly could not, protect her.

Every Sunday, her mother would go outside the house, leaving her father inside, and then she would send Maria in to take a cup of water to her father. Maria reported that every Sunday, for years, he would perform sexual acts on her and force her to do the same to him in return. Maria said that he would beat her, and she could only freeze because she was so scared and helpless as a little girl. She grew up with the message that she was a "bad girl" and felt she could not do anything to stop this.

In addition, she was sexually abused by her paternal grandfather, who began only four months after her father started abusing her, and it would happen in the same small house where her family lived, knowing that her brothers were right next door. The male authority figures in her life took advantage of her over and over. Maria stated that in order to cope with this, she would stab her doll over and over and imagine it was them. When she saw a dead animal or meat in the market, she would imagine it as her father and grandfather. This was the only way she knew how to handle the pain that she was going through. *She would picture them dead.*

Maria completed six years of education and described her school age years as a nightmare also as children would call her names. She said she felt "different" than the other children. But then she thought she had made a friend, and at age eleven, a girl from the school took her to her house. She was so happy that she finally had a friend until the girl took her clothes off. Maria exclaimed that she *froze* and then decided that she never more could trust *anybody* and would just have no friends.

At age fourteen, her mother married her off to a man who was twenty-two years old and who had already been divorced and already had a child. Maria married him to get away from her home life, but soon, he began to bring other women into the home. Her husband gave her to two of his man friends for sex one time, and she was beaten and sexually abused by them.

She tried to leave this man because he would sleep with other women in front of her and in front of the children (ages seven, eight, and nine). Once, he took her to a dark place and poured beer all over her, and she was so scared but could not escape. He told other people that she was just a prostitute and sold drugs, neither of which was true.

One day, Maria's husband gave her a soda to drink, laced with drugs, and she woke up two days later in a hotel. She was twenty-five years old at the time. She did not know where she was and screamed until a cleaning lady came to help her. She hurt all over, and she found that her whole body was bruised and bloody. Her back, stomach, arms, and legs were bitten and scratched. She had been raped repeatedly and could not walk. She was taken to the doctor, and the doctor stated that she must have been raped by three or four men. When she went home, her husband told her that she had been sold for drugs. During this incident, someone had hit her so hard that a tooth had been broken, and she showed me this as she cried in my office.

She continued to try to escape her husband, and he continued to look for her. Even the police would assault her and would not protect her from the domestic abuse. Her husband would wait for her on the street and beat her more. One day, she arrived home completely bloody from one of those beatings. She tried to leave him, but he kept finding her. She feared for her life. She was with this man for eleven years.

Maria stated that her children were starving, and she was trying so hard to stay away from her husband. She found a job cooking and working in a bar and brothel. She would cook and give clothes to abused women there, clean, serve dinner, care for children, and do anything she could to help the girls in the building. She always felt sick, vomiting, because of what she remembered and what she saw happening to the women there, but she wanted to do anything she could to help relieve them of their pain. She said that it was very hard to work there, but at least, her children were finally able to eat and go to school with shoes to wear.

One day, her husband found her and the children and tried to burn the house down with her and the children inside. She said there was smoke everywhere. He put a burning couch in the doorway so that they could not escape and then he went out the window and stood there watching the house burn. She said the children were crying, and they still remember this today.

That was when she realized that she had to get to the United States in order to survive. She left her three children in Mexico with her sister and promised them that she would bring them up to be with her in one year. She managed to keep her word; she worked hard and borrowed money to bring her children to the United States to be with her.

After moving to the United States, Maria slowly recovered, but the pain and scars are still there. She has since met a man who has provided a calm, peaceful, stable life for her, and the love that he has for her has helped her pull herself together as a woman worthy of love as well as provide a healthy father figure for her grown children. He has been supportive of her and has been able to nurture and care for her over the past years that they have known each other. According to Maria, he has been a *rock* for her during this time together and is always able to comfort her through her many symptoms of *post-traumatic stress disorder.*

Maria continues to have nightmares, is hypervigilant, and startles easily. She experiences extreme caution wherever she goes and does not like to leave the house without her husband with her. She experiences intrusive thoughts and triggers that are often uncomfortable and even painful, but her current husband is there to comfort her. The triggers may cause anxiety and other associated emotions, and these, sometimes, turn into panic attacks and great emotional stress, but he is there to calm her.

Maria experiences flashbacks that haunt her and frequent nightmares that disturb her sleep night after night. She feels insecure when her husband is not with her, and the thoughts keep her vigilant and on the lookout for danger, both day and night. Any danger to her husband would be a devastating loss for Maria, one which would be extremely difficult or impossible for her to survive. For Maria, danger is always around the corner, but her husband is there to provide protection, security, and love for her.

It was difficult for Maria to participate in therapy as it brought up many bad memories. For some time, the memories were so bad that she was in anguish. However, she has continued therapy and has attended several groups for victims of abuse over the years.

She currently lives with her husband and her son. The men work in construction and welding, and Maria sells food, cakes, Christmas ornaments, hair brooches, and jewelry. Her husband has been very patient with her; when she becomes depressed, he comforts her. When she is angry, he gives her space.

One day, as I was talking to Maria about telling her story through this book, I thought out loud, "Why am I writing this book anyway?"

This is what she said, "Everyone will want to read this book because after they read my story, this book will give *hope* to other women who have lived what I have lived. Women will know that they are not alone in their misery and sorrow, and they will know that other people are suffering with them and have been able to find help and solace. I have been able to work through my abuse and am a better person and can now help other people who have experienced the same thing, and for that, I am grateful".

She continued to talk about suffering. She said, "When I see someone with a sad face, and I feel that they are passing through something horrible, I just come out and tell them, 'I am poor. I have been raped and I have been beaten and I have been abused and I have starved, but I am all right now. We can talk about it.' And I know that they can come away feeling like they are not alone. There is help for women out there.

"The rich do not know what it is like to not even have $5 to their name, or to have $10 and have to try to only spend half of what they have so that they will always have some cash on them. The rich do not understand what it is like to move up from *nothing* in order to have *something*. The poor *do* understand what this feels like and, for this reason, understands the importance of love and compassion toward others who are hurting. Those who have *everything* look at other things differently."

Maria has sought treatment for her and her children since 2004. Many can attest to the pain that she experienced. Her husband is a hard worker and has been able to support the family throughout the years. He works every day, he pays his taxes, and he has not had any problems with the law except when he was a teenager, which contin-ues to haunt him. They are both trying so hard for over sixteen years to obtain legal status *through the legal process* and required paperwork and still have not acquired even a work permit. Her children and grandchildren are here in the United States, and now she feels she cannot return because she loves them and wants to be near the only family that she has. She and her husband continue to live in fear every day of being sent back to their country. They pray that this will never happen.

I do not believe Maria would have survived this separation. And for those who have a problem with deportees returning. I still believe that our attention and efforts for immigration reform need to be at fixing the root problem, not at trying to deport law-abiding families in the United States who are doing everything right to provide for their families. Is there a way to divide the good from the bad? Every situation is different, but we must listen to the families and the mothers and fathers, the children, and men and women who are seeking asylum. Each situation is individual. Until we solve the root problem, there will always be asylum seekers.

Give me your tired, your poor, your huddled
masses yearning to breathe free. (Emma Lazarus
sonnet, quoted on the Statue of liberty)

CHAPTER 14

Traveling across the Border

Often, clients will tell me their stories of courage in coming to the United States. I have great respect for those who had the strength and courage to make the trip, knowing that the trip is very dangerous and that people are dying every day as they try to make their way across the dessert or across the river, by foot or by vehicle, and by legitimate visas that turn into overstay. I understand that they come without following procedure, but it is almost impossible to obtain a visa before travelling as I have been told by many immigrants.

Men, women, and children alike do not always tell their families that they are leaving for fear someone may stop them. The stories of children who have run away are the most difficult to listen to. Almost always, they feel alone, unloved, and unprotected because their parents are already in the United States. They long to be with their parents and vice versa. Others are helped among family members, and this is where the gray area is and why children come to the United States without their parents unaccompanied.

I have heard stories of the indigenous people who *do not even know what the United States is*, but that there is work there and safety. They have only heard that they can feed their families or help their family by sending money back home. Since they do not trust officials or police, or perhaps because there are no police in their area, it is even harder for them to follow that protocol. So people just come on faith that it is a place that will provide safety and employment. I do not think they are even aware of an application for asylum process, and if they do, many are illiterate and would not be able to complete the application.

Ana reported that she came to the United States alone with her baby. She said she traveled from Tapachula, Mexico (near the Guatemalan border), all the way to the United States border alone. She stated that she did not bring any papers, only her daughter. *She said that she asked for help from God, and she feels this is the only reason she arrived safely.*

Ana reported that on the border, she went over the river and was caught by immigration and taken to the detention center. She only had a telephone number of her cousin in North Carolina, and her cousin became responsible for her. At first, she thought they were going to send her back to Guatemala, but then they said she was going to the United States. They let her go with no money or food, but a kind stranger gave her food and warmth. A lady from immigration told her that her cousin had paid the bus ticket, so she felt relieved. Ana reported that she is happy here, and things are not happening to her as they did in Guatemala and Mexico.

The stories I have heard are very similar in nature. The immigrants from the south travel by foot, train, and bus to even reach the Mexican-United States border, only to be sent back to their country over and over again. Immigrants from Guatemala, El Salvador, Honduras, and other countries often learn the Mexican lingo so that, just in case they are sent back, they are only sent back to Mexico and not all the way back to their native country which could be hundreds of miles away.

The ability to make it over the border is very difficult, but they continue to try even if it is costing them thousands of dollars. They are desperate. They tell me the risk of staying where they are is *more dangerous* than the risk of coming over the border. People are asked to pay their guide up to $8,000 in order to get help to bring them through to the other side. Many come as a family unit now because they are told that it may be easier to enter with children and because it may be cheaper (family rate). They normally do not have the money up front and promise to pay back loans from other people in order to make the trip. Sometimes, they sell a piece of land so that they will have the money to hire a guide. Several years ago, the cost was much less, but today, the cost is climbing significantly. All the individuals have courage, strength, and determination to do what they have done, and almost all are immigrating out of desperation.

Carla stated that she was very young when she and her mother and brother began their travel to the United States. She said that even traveling from Guatemala to Mexico was very difficult. She said when they finally had some money, they travelled slowly from Guatemala through Mexico, her mother trying to earn money all along the way so that they could eat.

Carla said that immigration of Mexico returned them to Guatemala many times, and so the last time, they returned in a cargo train, not as a passenger but in the cargo area. They called it the *tren de la muerte* (the train of death). She reported that the train was going, and they were running to catch up with it. Once inside, the door shut, and they could not breathe. She was only eight years old and was traveling with her brother who was about twelve years old and their mother. She stated that there were a lot of people in the cargo train. This all happened in Tapachula, Mexico, which is near the Guatemalan border.

Carla explained that they were in Mexico for several months and then they tried to pass from Mexico over the border to the United States. The first time they tried to pass, she said that she could not keep walking, so her mother took them back to the Mexican side. The second time, they were able to reach Brownsville, Texas, but they sent them all back to Mexico. The third time they tried, they walked for three to four days in the dessert. She stated that it was terrible; there were sexual assaults by predators, and there were snakes, wolves, scorpions, cactus, and sticky bushes. She remembers seeing dead bodies. They finally arrived in the United States on November 25, 2000.

Carla stated that they finally arrived at a house in the United States, and there was a lot of bad behavior by men who were hitting the children and the mothers. Then the guide took them from Texas to Tennessee. She explained that this was a very scary period because they put about fifty people inside a semitruck, and she thought they were all going to die. There were fumes from the truck and people urinating inside the truck because no one could get out. She was in the corner of the truck, trying to breathe through a small crack. Finally, she reported, outside, the police suspected something and opened the doors.

Carla explained that the police told the driver to follow them "because they are all going to be deported," but during the ride, the police went one way, and the driver went another way. Carla said she was allowed to ride up front at that time because she was one of the youngest there, but they were able to get away.

After leaving the semitruck, she said they were all put into a trailer where there were cockroaches and rats and other bugs. From there, they were taken to Delaware. In Delaware, things did not get much better as they were living in an apartment building that later burned to the ground, and again, they were homeless. She said the worst part about that was that "we had all of our savings (cash) under our mattress, and all the money burned up in the fire." They were not aware, nor did they understand, that they would be able to open a savings account in a local bank. In fact, I believe one needs a social security number for that anyway. Carla stated that she was about fifteen years old when that happened.

There has been much conflict over whether there will be a wall built on the Mexican-USA border. Mr. Schey, President for the Center for Human Rights & Constitutional Law, wrote an article that discussed the issue of a wall being build on the southern border of the United States. Following are parts of a letter from Peter Schey, President, Center for Human Rights and Constitutional Law, December 24, 2018 (used by permission) who has represented several million undocumented immigrants in class action cases over the past forty years.[7] It reads:

A summary of this article (Mr. Schey) explains that several million undocumented immigrants in class-action cases over the past

---

[7]   Schey, Peter, Center for Human Rights and Constitutional Law, "The Stupidest Government Shutdown in History," December 23, 2018.

forty years have been represented and interviewed about why and how immigrants came to the United States. Based on these conversations, he found that a large number never made the dangerous journey sneaking across the southern border but entered the country concealed in vehicles through the main ports of entry (Otay Mesa, San Ysidro, Calexico, Brownsville, and Eagle Pass.) Many of the cars are never inspected. President Trump has never proposed allocating funds to make modern technology available at ports of entry to reduce migration (or drugs) in concealed vehicles. This just doesn't have the "visceral appeal of a 'border wall'" that people like.

He states that in speaking with immigrants, about half entered the United States with temporary visas, developed ties to stay and then decided to stay. However, the president has not advocated for funding for the development of improved programs to track whether visitors timely depart when their visas expire.

He also reports that most of these immigrants are not from Central America or Mexico. Most come from European or Asian countries and will arrive in airplanes flying right over the wall President Trump wants to build.

He reports that thousands of immigrants pay smugglers to lead a journey across the border, and others may pay a pilot to fly small groups of migrants to remote landing strips in the US. These smugglers can make thousands of dollars easily, by charging outrageous prices to a vulnerable population. This is convenient way for the smugglers in a land where there is very little opportunity for employment. Others have paid a boat captain to bring them in by sea. Others flew to a third country where they did not need a visa or could easily obtain one via Canada.

Also, another critical fact that no wall will address is that those fleeing extreme forms of violence and others seeking to be united with husbands, wives, or children here will do almost anything to get across the border. "Their determination is so strong, and the drive for family unity so powerful that they will find ways to get over, under, or around, any wall President Trump may build. As former Secretary of the Department of Homeland Security Janet Napolitano once said, 'You show me a 50-foot wall, and I'll show you a 51-foot ladder.'"

Schey went on to explain that there are other ways to control the borders: allow the *caravanistas* to apply as "refugees" entering the country; allow for funding for immigration lawyers and asylum officers to help process the backlog of applications for asylum (now backlogged about four years) and three quarters of a million people—all waiting in the United States for an answer. Second, since the Trump Administration is denying 75 percent of the asylum cases due to refusal of domestic violence and gang violence, it inspires asylees to forget the application process and come in illegally. This needs to be addressed. Third, approve DACA applicants (over a million) to remain in the United States and become citizens since they have lived here all their lives. This would allow university students to take professional jobs (doctors, nurses, social workers, etc.) which are high in demand now, have a path to citizenship. They have already been here all their lives anyway and are "Americanized."

Raul is a twenty-seven-year-old DACA recipient and currently has a work permit, which enables him to work. He was telling me about his story as an undocumented youth. He states that he was always a very good student and was able to graduate high school in 2011. Before he received DACA status, he was not able to get a driver's license. He was able to take the driving course, and he passed the written test, but he was not able to take the driving test because he did not have a birth certificate.

After high school, he wanted to get into the marines, but he was turned down over and over because he needed to be at least a permanent resident. His dream was to join the aviation section of the marines, but they kept turning him down. So he started taking classes at the local community college and started on an associate's degree. His plan was to graduate and continue in the Aviation and Science Bachelor's program as a professional pilot through the University of Maryland, Eastern Shore. He could not afford more than one class at a time, because, as an undocumented immigrant, he had to pay "out-of-state tuition." He only attended two years, part time, because of the high cost.

In the meantime, his parents returned to Guatemala to care for their elderly parents, leavening Raul in the United States. Since he could not travel back and forth, he decided to stay and apply for DACA status. He met his girlfriend who he eventually married. He joined the Melfa Flying Club and started taking flying lessons at $185.00 an hour. He also paid $2,000 to join the club, and he was very motivated to become a pilot. He took the required training hours, but when it was time to fly solo, he was not able to do so without a birth certificate or passport. He was shut down again.

Because of his great motivation, he decided to follow another career goal. He eventually received DACA and now has a social security card, work permit, driver's license, and he can drive and pay taxes. He now owns his own business. He said, "When the doors are shut, you go through the windows."

Andrea said that she came from a remote area in Guatemala and spoke the Mam dialect. She loved her town, with the dirt roads and the outdoor market. She told me her grandmother wore the typical dress of the Mayan Indian and sold blouses and dresses to the city market. Andrea had been approached by several men who wanted her to go to work in the fields of *amapola* (poppy), but she knew that she did not want to go that route. She wanted to continue her education and be a teacher, but the path to the school was dangerous, and she feared for her life. She had relatives and a sister living in the United States, so she decided to go, taking a big chance on crossing the border.

She first went to St. George, Utah, and lived there for four months with relatives, but there was no work there. She then left for Delaware where she had a sister, and at first, she worked in the fields in Delaware and then began to work in the chicken plants. She and her husband now have a child and have been living here since 2005 and are happy and are living comfortably. She is applying for asylum, hoping that she may be able to obtain permission to travel back and forth between countries.

Andrea explains that she always misses her two children who she left behind in Guatemala, and this makes her very unhappy. She explains that her happiness is never complete. She and her husband have three children who were born in this country, but she misses her children in Guatemala. She, as many people explain, *would love to return to her country, but not without the ability to travel back and forth, since she has family in both countries now. Therefore, she feels "stuck" here.*

so many people tell me this. They WANT to be able to travel back to their country but know that they would not be able to travel back to the United States, so they decide to never leave the country. The visas are not handed out easily and are almost always denied. If undocumented here, there is no way to return here once out of the country without coming over the border again. And this is extremely difficult and dangerous.

Julio came in for therapy after surviving a deportation to Mexico where he had fallen into the hands of the drug cartels or gangs—this was not completely clear as his eyes were covered and no one identified themselves as being from a certain group. Julio had come to the United States as a five-year-old child, had gone to high school, and graduated along with his class. He wanted to go to college but could not do so for lack of papers and inability to apply for financial aid. He began working in construction and then met Andrea. When he was thirty-nine years old, he and Andrea decided to get married. Andrea had three children of her own who were grown and were beginning to form their own families.

Julio had been picked up for drinking when he was a teenager. At the time, he did not have a driver's license, which put him on alert with immigration. Twenty-five years later, ICE followed him to work one day and arrested him, although he had never gotten into trouble for the next twenty years. Julio went with them willingly and was placed in a detention center, later to be deported. While in the detention center, his wife frantically tried to get him out, got a lawyer and had several letters written on his behalf, explaining that he was a hard-working member of the community. He stayed longer than usual because he refused to sign deportation papers and with the help of his lawyer, he applied for asylum. He spoke English like a native American and was translating for others in the detention center and even encouraged others through his own faith, which provided hope for many. However, he eventually was deported. His wife thought she would die without him, and the whole family suffered his loss.

The bad thing is, that at the border, he was kidnapped. He has bought two pastries at a store and called his wife to see if she would send him some money so that he could travel to a relative's house. While in the store, two men grabbed his telephone, put something over his head, and threw him into a car. He did not know where he went. They put him in a house, and then they called his wife the next day and demanded that she send $10,000, or else he would be killed. She could hear them hitting him in the background and cursing, and she was heartbroken. He was her life, and America was his country.

The men continued to call her, cursing, and told her that if she did not send the money, they were going to *cut him into pieces and put him in a box and send it to her house.* She said they called four times, and she had been advised not to admit that she knew him. Each time they called, she tried not to act emotional, but she recorded the line, and she noted the telephone numbers that they were using. Two of the numbers came from Arizona, one in California, one in Mexico, and one in Texas. She wrote them all down and tried not to cry or scream as she heard them beating him in the background.

The local police told her that they could not do anything because this was all happening in Mexico. She went to her lawyer, and the lawyer listened to the recording, but there was nothing she could do. The immigration lawyer had already been fighting for Julio, trying to get him out of the deportation hearing, to no avail. Then they did not call anymore.

I personally knew this family, and as his wife talked to me, I, too, was devastated and hurting for the family. They had been living in the United States for over twenty years and now had children and grandchildren. They were working hard and minding their own business. But Andrea cried because her husband had told her "he would never leave her," and she just felt that he would come back. In her denial, she could not accept that he had been killed.

The next week, Julio miraculously called and said he had been released. He went to Monterey and then eventually, two months later, he was able to make his way back to his family on the eastern shore. He told his wife that the men had beat him only when they were on the phone with his wife. He always had his eyes covered and never saw anything. He remembers that after a few days, they said they were going to kill him and took him in a car. But when he walked through the house, he felt that there were dead bodies there, and he was stepping on the bodies because there were many.

Then, someone said, "Leave him here, leave him. He does not have family—throw him out. They could not verify that he had family in the United States.

I was one of the therapists who had been talking to his wife during this ordeal. I cried with her as she cried, I prayed hard when we did not know what was happening, and I rejoiced with her when she heard that he was alive.

The world is tough. He found out that the people in the Mexican store where he was calling from, was working with the cartel and had given them the telephone number that Julio was using. He came back but will be forever a changed man.

Another woman told me that crossing the border was a bad experience for her. She had come in 2004 with her two children—one was three years old, and the other one was one year and six months. During the trip, she became separated from the children, and someone else took them in a truck which was less risky for little children. When she crossed, she was told that her three-year-old daughter was missing. She went to the consulate and begged for them to find her. She was found at an office near the border, but then she had been deported back to Mexico, and her other daughter was still somewhere in the United States. So she crossed over again in order to get her younger daughter who was in Tucson. Her older daughter had been lost for two days, and her younger daughter for four days.

This woman explained to me that it was common for mothers to turn the youngest children over to someone who could drive them across the border because it was safer. Then on the other side, they usually reunite. I'm not sure how this works logistically, and this was years ago. Her husband was already here and waited for her. He had saved all his money to bring his family to join him; another example of chain migration.

Many people are abused on the trip to the United States. Several of our women were raped while being escorted to the United States by the "coyotes" or guides. They end up having the children and caring for them with love. One patient came with her boyfriend. The patient's boyfriend disappeared during the night, after the smugglers had threatened to rape his girlfriend, and he had defended her. She fears that they murdered him.

Inez told me that the person who brought her and her children told them that everything would be good, and no one would be hurt. But in Tapachula, they got into the car and were taken to a train. Then they were told to get on TOP of the train. She said it was raining a lot, and she had her two children—one age seven, and the other one was eleven years old. She said that the children were crying, and there were other people with babies on top of the train. She said the train was going so fast! She said that someone tried to separate her from her children and people offered to take the children in a car, but she said NO. She said, "I don't care what happens, but I will never give up my children!"

After the train, they got in a car and were taken to Nogales. The guide told them to go away, but in Nogales, immigration put them into a detention center where they stayed two days and then were transported to another place where it was *really cold*. (Everyone tells me the place is very cold!) She said they had separated many children from their parents, and she said, "NO! NO! NO! That will not happen to us!"

Even though it was cold in the holding area, she said one feels safe there and able to rest. She said the children were crying. Luckily, she did not see anyone die. Although safely in the United States, she said that she had been humiliated and had suffered much hatred and discrimination. But she said, "Yes, there may be some bad people at the border and entering the United States, but most of the people are good that comes here. It took twelve days to go from Guatemala to Delaware. God is the one that helps us."

Imagine that...God is helping the immigrant enter the United States, and our presidents are trying to take them out and make them face death in their country!

It is very interesting to hear the stories of travels to the United States. One thing everyone says is that they are glad that immigration has found them, or else they would have died in the dessert or been assaulted by some bad person. Another thing they say is that the *holding area is very cold.* They are usually assisted as they explain their stories of violence, crime, and abuse from their country. They say that people who have helped them are very kind. They have risked their lives and given up everything they own in order to escape death in their countries.

But not everyone is "nice." *Maricela* stated that she spent seven or eight days travelling to get to the United States before she was stopped by immigration. Her sisters and her son were with her, and they had no food or water when they were found. When they were found, the border control shouted at her and treated her really bad, and she cried. She knows that they did not understand what she had been through.

Maricela stated that she was only seventeen years old at the time, but a woman there kept accusing her of lying about her age because she appears older than her age. She cried that she was seeking refuge and consolation, but everyone was mean and angry at her. They did not even offer her a glass of water. She had been walking all night and was so hungry and thirsty.

She said that while in the "jail," *it was so cold.* There were no blankets, and they had taken her shoes. They made them throw everything away. She said there were 120 children in a small room. There was only one bathroom and no water, and children were drinking water out of the toilets.

Then she said they were transferred to another jail in Arizona where they stayed for four days. She found a guard there who was kind enough to bring some food and water. Then the Guatemalan consulate came. She had not bathed in nine days, so they then allowed her to bathe and gave her five vaccinations. They were finally able to get water. They stayed another three days and then were put on a bus and taken to a holding center where there was toothpaste, crafts, exercise, English classes, TV, and lunch. She stayed there twenty-four days and then was taken to Delaware to join the rest of her family.

Maricela reported that she now attends the Adventist School in Baltimore, Rescate, one day a month from 9:00 a.m.—3:00 p.m. She is studying to become a first-aid volunteer and is learning how to survive a natural disaster. She hopes to get a diploma for this. She is also studying English. Maricela reported that she used to give presentations and believes herself to be a good speaker. She hopes to further her education in other ways in the future.

She earns some money by providing childcare for her friends and neighbors. She attends the Adventist church and has cousins and brothers in the area. She also has her sister who is now living in another state.

So often, this is the story of the younger people. They do not feel there are any other options. They have never lived in peace. For these people living in the hills of Guatemala, their world is only what they see around them. But then they hear of a place called the United States. They hear that it is very dangerous to get there, and it costs thousands of dollars (or in their case, *quetzals*), but they are told that in this country, there is no hunger, men are punished for hitting women, and police are not bribed. There is the opportunity to work, to make money, to buy their own house, and to support their own parents or relatives in their country. For this, they are forever grateful, and they never cease to give thanks to God who has been with them all the way.

It is concerning to me that Christians do not take the Gospel seriously. Father James Martin, SJ said, "Even Pope Francis said, 'A person who thinks only about building walls, wherever they may be, and not building bridges, is not Christian. This is not the Gospel.' Christianity is about helping the stranger, even if it carries risk. Jesus is speaking to you from the Gospels. It is Christ whom we turn away when we build walls. It is Christ whom we reject when we slash quotas for refugees. It is Christ whom we are killing by letting them die in poverty and war rather than opening our door."[8] That's what the Parable of the Good Samaritan is all about.

---

[8] Martin, James, S.J., "I Was a Stranger and You Did Not Welcome Me," January 27, 2017.

Let us never tire of preaching love, it is
the force that will overcome the world.
(Oscar Romero)

CHAPTER 15

Social Work with Immigrants—
Treating the Trauma

As Peace Corps volunteers, we were taught during orientation that the acculturation process is very difficult in going to another country and then returning. The trainers told us that, upon return, our friends and family would probably not really identify or understand our experience in another country, nor would they really care that much. I remember that going to Ecuador, for me, was easy. I adapted right away to living with a latrine as a bathroom, no hot water, and electricity only at certain times of the day. But returning from Ecuador, it was a very different story. I remember being repulsed by the richness of the people at the airport, the gluttony of people eating more than they possibly needed, and the waste created while people threw good and useful things out for no reason except that it was not needed any longer. I could only think of the poverty that I had been immersed in while living in another country. I remember standing and looking at the microwave in amazement, feeling the hot water coming out of a faucet, and a stove that would immediately warm up. It took me about one year to finally accept the life as it was in the United States again.

In working with the immigrant community and listening to their stories and their hardships, I cannot help but put myself in their shoes. It must be extremely hard to come to a country where they may be discriminated against, looked down on, and criticized for not speaking English. I wonder how they are coping with this. We have had acculturation support groups for these individuals, and I remember understanding what they were saying; they had come here thinking that they would be here temporarily, only to find out later that they were stuck here. In the beginning of their journey, they would be excited and amazed at the differences in the cultures and thrilled that they could finally work, even without a work permit. They could feed their families and support their mother back home. And then suddenly, there would be a big bout of depression because they one day realize that they may not be able to return, that they were here to stay. Then they miss their loved ones, their country, and they wish that they could travel back and forth, but this is impossible at this point.

I currently am employed as a therapist at a health clinic and at a domestic violence shelter for women and children, and there are many who come through the office with problems dealing with physical health, mental health and prenatal issues. To set the record clear, undocumented immigrants are not eligible, in any state that I know of, for Medicaid, food stamps, or public assistance, and they cannot purchase health care through the marketplace (this may be changing in some states). In the clinic that I work at, they ALL pay cash on a sliding fee basis. If they need a specialist, they must also pay full price. When they go to the emergency room, they are sent a bill, and for this reason, they avoid going to the doctor or hospital at all costs except to have a baby. There is financial emergency assistance for those having a baby, and there are a few other programs to help them manage their medical treatment, but government assistance is not an option for them.

In 2010, I worked with thirteen immigrant children ages two to five years old, who had been sexually abused by Dr. Earl Bradley, a pediatrician from Lewes, Delaware, who had been indicted on 471 charges of molesting, raping, and exploiting at least 103 child patients. He was charged with first-degree rape, sexual exploitation of a child by photo film, and endangering the welfare of a child. His victims ranged in age from three months to thirteen years old. He had abused over 130 confirmed cases of preschool children by use of cameras. He used toys and Disney mechanical rides to lure the children into the basement of his office and a building outside the office which included cartoon and Disney characters. I used Preschool PTSD Treatment (PPT) therapy with these immigrant children whose mothers were only Spanish speaking and unaware but trusting of the doctor with the respect that a normal parent would usually give a pediatrician. Today, mothers are still bringing their daughters in for therapy and continue to grieve in despair and guilt for bringing their children to this doctor. He is now serving fourteen life sentences. PPT was used to treat children from ages 3-6 who were verbal enough to work with their memories of abuse by Dr. Bradley. This is an example of how immigrant families are taken advantage of when vulnerable and unable to understand the laws of the country and afraid to report injustices for fear of being deported.

From one clinician to another, recognizing past trauma in a patient is essential in diagnosing and treating of an individual. Before making any diagnosis—ADHD, conduct disorder, oppositional defiant disorder, OCD, depression, anxiety, autism, and a number of other mental health illnesses—find out what trauma they have experienced in their lives, or rule out trauma as a reason for their symptoms. Ask about their childhood; was it happy or was it full of fear and violence? Ask about their lives as a teenager and young adult. Ask about their first loves, their intimate relationships, as well as relationships with their parents. Natural disasters, car accidents, physical operations, sexual abuse, etc. could be indicators for the behaviors they present with. Then treat the trauma first.

The different therapies that I use to treat trauma are primarily:

- EFT (Emotional Feeling Technique). Gary Craig—best treatment for immediate results, used for panic and anxiety by tapping on certain places throughout the body, points of energy known as meridians. This technique can calm a person immediately and is a process that they can take home with them and use between sessions.
- EMDR (Eye Movement Desensitization and Reprocessing). Francine Shapiro—helps with reduction of nightmares,

flashbacks, grief, rape, emotional, physical, or sexual abuse, and a wide range of past traumatic events that is causing distress in a person's life.

- TANT (Traumatic Art Narrative Therapy). Dr. Lyndra Bills—helps reduce intrusive symptoms of depression and anger from a trauma, helps those who have difficulty verbalizing traumatic events by using drawings to tell the narrative and provide resolution to traumatic experiences.
- Preschool PTSD Treatment (PPT). Michael S. Scheeringa, MD, MPH—a CBT-based therapy that is very effective in treating children between the ages of three to six, as was used in the case of the pediatrician who abused hundreds of children.

Other therapies are intertwined with the abovementioned therapies, such as play therapy, Trauma-Focused Cognitive Behavioral Therapy, hypnosis, regression therapy (Brian L. Weiss, MD) and various meditative and relaxation exercises, but each therapist has to find what works best for them.

Along with treatment for physical and emotional distress, one must also consider the basic necessities of life: food, water, housing, and health. Many immigrants have pulled together their resources in order to survive. It is common to see one family per room in a house, sharing food and resources with the rest of the household. There is what one would call "warm beds," in which workers take turns sleeping in the same bed, keeping the bed warm both day and night. The immigrants place immigration processes at the top of their priority list and are saving all that they have to pay immigration application fees. They do not hesitate to "pay the price" for lawyers, fees for transportation to essential appointments, and bonds to be released from jails when picked up for deportation, which can go into the thousands of dollars. Family and friends will come together to help with these high costs because this is a priority for them, that they be able to remain in the United States with loved ones.

Children are the most vulnerable of the vulnerable. The primary focus, as it would be for any parent, is the health and welfare of their child. To create a bond with any client, take interest in their children and assist them with information on how to help educate their child, feed their child, and improve their relationship with their child. They will be grateful for the information. They love their children more than anything in the world; any parent will understand that, and to have support from a counselor or friend in the United States will mean the world to them. To have a family separated from their children is the most traumatic and cruel event that could happen to them.

Food, clothing, and housing are important; and as a social worker, it is understood that before a person can be healthy, emotionally, one must have these elements taken care of. In spite of the poverty (what we might think is poverty), most immigrants give thanks for all of the blessings in their lives, and they will share whatever they have with a stranger. And although they are compassionate and would do anything to help a neighbor, they struggle from day to day. It is important to consider the immigrant's basic needs while determining treatment that is needed.

In speaking with Colleen, the agency midwife, there are instances of difficulty for those who are currently living in the United States. One of those stories was of a woman who had come in a few days after her C-section. She had an infection of the skin covering most of her face and could not afford to go for care. She was in such pain because she could not afford the pain pills that had been prescribed. When she was given a ride home, the woman who transported her, who also worked at the clinic, found out that she and her family were sleeping on the floor and using coats as blankets. If the home would have had sanitary conditions, she would not have gotten the infection. Since she was undocumented, she completely depended on her family and our clinic to help her with the most basic of needs.

Another patient had a miscarriage but could not afford an emergency room visit and, therefore, did not go to the hospital. She developed such a bad infection that she spent over a month in the hospital, most of it in the ICU. Since she could not obtain health insurance and would have to pay out of pocket for medical care, the fear of a high hospital bill kept her from getting emergency medical care when she needed it most. Giving a client a work permit while waiting (four years) for their asylum case to be approved (or denied) would help solve the problem of lack of medical care. Allowing anyone to purchase a health care plan, I would think, helps the economy as well as the individual in need of services.

The houses that the patients rent are not always the best because the landlords fail to repair and replace plumbing and electric, carpets, and broken structural items of the house. They are often unsafe, with broken windows and locks. One day, a mother came into the office with roaches coming out of the baby's car seat and running through the office. It took several of us to catch them, step on them, and spray to get rid of them. She said she could not afford to have an exterminator come in to treat for bugs.

A nurse said she went to do a home visit with a family that was living in a trailer park. The trailer had a huge hole in the middle of the floor in the kitchen area, and grass was growing up through it. When it rained, the water would come through the holes in the ceiling.

The undocumented agricultural workers are still traveling from state to state to work in the fields and continue to worry about being taken away from their families. One woman recently told me that she was at home one day when ICE (immigration) came to her house seeking her husband. She knew where he was, but he was hidden, and since they could not find him, they decided to take her in, which they were not really authorized to do because she had done nothing wrong. She cried as she described the scariest feeling in her life as the immigration officer yelled at her for forty minutes as they took her to the Dover office in handcuffs, yelling obscenities in her face, practically pushing their fingers into her nose and face, pressuring to tell them where her husband was. She said she remained silent but was terrified as they put her into a cell, only later to be released, just in time to pick her children up from school. She was not only treated for trauma from her country but worse trauma from the United States.

I appreciate the Latino population so much, and I feel like they have given me so much more than I have given them. They have told me that I have a Latina heart, and I do believe that! There is something about the culture that makes me feel closely connected to them. The people that I have met are spiritual and carry a tradition of faith within them, that God will help them through any situation. They are also the most generous in sharing with their friends and family. I have learned that the poorer a person is, the more giving they are.

As I traveled to Guatemala, Nicaragua, El Salvador, Ecuador, Mexico, etc., I realize more and more that we have so much to be thankful for in the United States. I saw a quote once that said, "Imagine that God gave you today only that which you had given thanks for yesterday." This makes me even more conscious of all the blessings that we have every day. It also reminds me of the call for us to do what we can to share our "wealth" with others.

A Mexican American friend of mine had her own traumatizing experience to tell, and she has always lived in the United States. She told me that she had been attacked physically and emotionally by other Americans in this country although she had been born here. Her Mexican American family has been terrorized and discriminated against, humiliated, and looked down upon, just because she looks Mexican. She stated that her children are graduating from high school, and she has taught them the traditions of her cultural background. But she still experiences men in trucks telling her to "go home" as she walks down the street. She experiences discrimination even as she visits her husband's grave in the community cemetery because of her race.

Another Mexican American friend found out that her relatives in Mexico had been kidnapped just because they are assumed to have money from "rich" relatives in the United States. Several of her family members in Mexico had to leave their hometown because of death threats and extortion. They had experienced kidnappings, death threats, and torture. Everyone is living in fear today.

Adapting to the American culture is challenging because mixed within the acculturation is the discrimination and racism that is present in our society. Leaving everything behind in search of refuge is not easy. Everyone wants to live in a better world with basic needs met. It is up to you and me to be mindful of our ability to serve and to have compassion for those in need. We have the ability to use our influence to address the hatred and violence in the world and to change the bad into the good. And then, we can see a hopeful future for everyone.

Dios te bendiga.

ABOUT THE AUTHOR

Phyllis "Yvonne" Dodd, LCSW lives in Greensboro, Maryland and is an employee of La Red Health Center and the Mid-Shore Council on Domestic Violence as a licensed bilingual clinical social worker. She works primarily with Latino families in the area of domestic violence and childhood sexual trauma. Phyllis is a graduate of Juniata College and studied her junior year abroad in Barcelona, Spain, through Brethren Colleges Abroad. She began her work in Ecuador as a Peace Corps volunteer and has continued to build her social work skills over the years. She completed her masters in social work from the University of Maryland in Baltimore.

Phyllis has provided treatment for male offenders of domestic violence for several years and considers this a part of her role as peacemaker duties. She provides parenting classes in Spanish and has worked exclusively with immigrant preschool children sexually abused by pediatrician E. Bradley in 2010 and has become experienced in treating very small children.

Her work with the Church of the Brethren has included work with refugee resettlement, the district Peace and Justice Committee, and Brethren Peace Fellowship. She has written a curriculum called "The 10 Commandments of Wellness for Use in Church Settings" (printed by the Church of the Brethren, Elgin, ILL). In doing so, she has helped individuals seek better ways of taking care of themselves in holistic ways. In her spare time, she enjoys playing guitar and doghouse bass with her bluegrass band.

Her goal now is to help asylum applicants obtain legal status in the United States by helping them tell their stories. She has found that her passion for peace and justice in the world is her premise for all that she does to work for those who are voiceless.

For more information, you can contact Phyllis at *pydodd@gmail.com*

CPSIA information can be obtained
at www.ICGtesting.com
Printed in the USA
FSHW011832061020
74466FS